THE

COURAGEOUS
MESSENGER

HOW TO
SUCCESSFULLY
SPEAK UP AT WORK

KATHLEEN D. RYAN
DANIEL K. OESTREICH
GEORGE A. ORR III

Jossey-Bass Publishers • San Francisco

Substantial discounts on bulk quantities of Jossey-Bass books are available to corporations, professional associations, and other organizations. For details and discount information, contact the special sales department at Jossey-Bass Inc., Publishers (415) 433–1740; Fax (800) 605–2665.

For sales outside the United States, please contact your local Simon & Schuster International Office.

Manufactured in the United States of America

Library of Congress Cataloging-in-Publication Data

Ryan, Kathleen, date.
  The courageous messenger : how to successfully speak up at work /
  Kathleen D. Ryan, Daniel K. Oestreich, George A. Orr III.
    p. cm.— (The Jossey-Bass business & management series)
  Includes index.
  ISBN 0–7879–0268–3
  1. Communication in organizations. 2. Interpersonal
communication. 3. Management—Employee participation. 4. Courage.
5. Assertiveness (Psychology). I. Oestreich, Daniel K., date.
II. Orr, George A., date. III. Title. IV. Series.
HD30.5.R93 1996
650.1—dc20   96–26632

Interior Design by Suzanne Pustejovsky Design, Austin, Texas

FIRST EDITION

HB Printing   10 9 8 7 6 5 4 3 2 1

The Jossey-Bass

Business & Management Series

EDGES

When we walk to the edge

of all the light we have

and take the step into the

darkness of the unknown,

we must believe one of

two things will happen—

There will be something solid

for us to stand on,

or we will be taught

how to fly.

—Claire Morris

CONTENTS

ACKNOWLEDGMENTS

First and foremost, we have a deep appreciation for the messengers who shared their stories with us. Their compelling examples inspired us to write a book that would pass along their insights and courage. The title of this book is really a dedication to them.

Our thanks go to the many friends, colleagues, and clients who have offered us advice and support as we wrote. Generously, they gave us hours of their time as they critiqued our models, challenged our assumptions, and tactfully suggested ways to improve. Their honest criticisms and unflagging support over three years make this book much finer than what our work alone would ever have produced. They were all wonderful messengers to us.

A few members of this prized support network deserve special thanks. Reviewing our manuscript were Wendy Dittamore, Carl Griffin, Benita Horn, Barbara Hummel, Mike Plummer, Wayne Sepolen, Bob Weyant, and Mary Ann Woodruff. Frank Basler, Michael Buschmohle, Stephanie Gordon-Cady, Marjorie Lepley, and Barbara Magusin went above and beyond in their reviews, devoting extra time to several follow-up conversations that resulted in true breakthroughs for us. We discovered that Wendy Dittamore and Anne Orr are more than family; without their enthusiasm and investigative skills, we would never have found Claire Morris. Peggy West offered us her time and talent as she willingly interviewed people about their messenger experiences. Many of the opportunities to speak to these people were due to the efforts of Donna Stringer. Gene Slape, the cyberdoc, in a category all his own, kept us on-line and thus on track.

We have a special sense of gratitude to those who are responsible for this publication. Byron Schneider, our editor at Jossey-Bass, gently pushed our thinking and helped us to refine our perspective time after time. His advocacy for our work is deeply appreciated. Ray Bard, our wise friend and talented book producer, gracefully guided our work past more than one tough spot. He has encouraged us to write this book since our very first conversation in 1988. And to Helen Hyams and Suzanne Pustejovsky, we owe great thanks for the extra effort that went into the editing and design of our material.

Finally, we want to acknowledge our debt to our families and closest friends for the time we stole from these important relationships to complete this book. Sarah Stiteler and children Tyler and Victoria deserve the Nobel Prize for Patience in their loving support for Dan and for our collective work.

June 1996   Kathleen D. Ryan
                                               Issaquah, Washington

                                               Daniel K. Oestreich
                                               Redmond, Washington

                                               George A. Orr III
                                               Issaquah, Washington

THE AUTHORS

Kathleen D. Ryan is a principal of Cultures for Quality, Inc., a consulting firm based near Seattle, Washington. She received her B.A. degree (1969) from the University of California at Berkeley in English and her M.A. degree (1978) from the University of Southern California in public administration.

Ryan is known for her work in turning fear-based organizations into ones characterized by trust and collaboration. She works with her clients to build organizational cultures in which quality can flourish. Joshua Hammond, former president of the American Quality Foundation, called Ryan one of a "handful of pioneering thinkers who are shaping the new world of quality. . . . [She is] an organizational consultant with an instinct for translating complex human behavior into practical concepts." Ryan maintains an extensive national consulting practice, often working with her husband and business partner, George Orr. She has served as both a member and director of the Organization Development Professional Practice Area for the American Society for Training and Development. Ryan is the coauthor, with Daniel K. Oestreich, of *Driving Fear Out of the Workplace: How to Overcome the Invisible Barriers to Quality, Productivity, and Innovation*. Published by Jossey-Bass in 1991, it received the Society for Human Resource Management's 1992 Book Award. In 1980, she coproduced the award-winning training film *The Workplace Hustle*.

Daniel K. Oestreich is also a principal of Cultures for Quality, Inc. He received his B.A. degree (1973) from Yale University in history and his M.A. degree (1975) from the University of Colorado at Boulder in guidance and counseling.

Oestreich focuses his consulting work on assisting private and public sector leaders with feedback, personal transformation, trust building, and team development. His favorite work combines the spirit of Jungian psychology with an ever-deepening respect for systems theory. He is the coauthor, with Kathleen D. Ryan, of *Driving Fear Out of the Workplace* and is a well-known speaker and presenter within the quality movement. His professional background includes many years as a personnel generalist for the City of Bellevue, Washington.

Oestreich is a former board member of the Eastside Quality Council and a member of the advisory board of *HR Newsletter*, a publication of the International City/County Management Association. He has written elsewhere on employee development and conflict management themes.

George A. Orr III is also a principal of Cultures for Quality, Inc. He received his B.A. degree (1968) from St. Lawrence University in sociology and his M.P.H. degree (1974) from the University of Hawaii School of Public Health.

Orr consults with businesses and organizations that are undergoing the stresses of change resulting from growth, resizing, and culture transformation. He helps his clients with planning and implementing change, strategic planning for quality improvement, team building, and the creation of vision. Working primarily in the service sector, Orr has the reputation of being a practical and intuitive facilitator who is able to help people feel comfortable with new approaches, take risks, and overcome their fears. He is particularly skilled in the role of a confidential sounding board for executives and managers who need some outside perspective.

Orr has previously held management positions in health care, human services, and manufacturing organizations. His last management role was as director of preventive care development and health promotion for Group Health Cooperative of Puget Sound.

PART I

EVERYDAY ACTS OF COURAGE

1

WELCOME
TO THIS
BOOK

THE COURAGEOUS MESSENGER is a guidebook for helping you to improve your ability to speak up at work. We believe that speaking up is one of the most important skills anyone can master to prepare for the workplace of the future—a future that has already begun.

This book is about *messengers,* people who:

- Feel a need to speak up or say something

- In order to positively influence the thinking, feelings, or behavior of others

- But hesitate because of a concern about personal risk or repercussions

The premise of this book is that those who do not know how to speak up can *learn* to do so. Those who already say what's on their mind can *improve* their skill and grace. By doing so, individuals will begin to build more positive workplace dynamics and relationships. They will be better able to address problems and positively influence change. And in the process, they will have the increased sense of satisfaction and personal integrity that comes from acting in a more honest, straightforward, and courageous way.

We are also writing for people who do not seem to need more courage. These are people who easily say what is on their mind but sense that they need more skill in the way they present and discuss their messages. These readers understand that the more effectively they bring forward a difficult issue, the more likely it is that they will get the results they seek.

We have planned this book to be personal and informal. As authors, we will frequently talk to you directly, challenging you with questions and suggesting that you apply points to your relationships. The focus will be the real world of messy human interactions. This means that we will include successes—as well as situations that did not work particularly well. We will not sugar-coat the difficulty or the risk involved with bringing a tough piece of news to someone else.

Many stories fill the pages ahead. They are drawn from our experiences as consultants and employees and from interviews with more than seventy people who shared their messenger stories with us. We hope the stories will help you to know that you are not alone in worrying about bringing forward sensitive issues. Those we interviewed taught us much and it is a pleasure to pass along their insights and learnings. The circumstances of their stories have been disguised to protect their privacy.

Who We Are

The three of us—Kathy Ryan, Dan Oestreich, and Bud Orr—have been in messenger situations many times. Over the years, we have personally struggled with the messenger's challenge: knowing when and how to bring up subjects that are sensitive, that might threaten or offend others, that might turn relationships sour. In our own past experiences, as employees or managers, we have all been faced with tough decisions about speaking up. And now, as consultants, we are frequently hired to say hard things to people, things that those inside an organization are reluctant to bring up.

In 1991, we published a book about the phenomenon of people not speaking up in organizations, called *Driving Fear Out of the Workplace*.[1] The main dynamics we described then have been confirmed over and over:

■ Seventy percent of those we surveyed before writing *Driving Fear Out of the Workplace* said that a fear of repercussions was one of the reasons they chose not to speak up about concerns. Many also said they believed it would do no good to speak up.

■ The most difficult subjects for people to talk about related to management practices.

■ People are very concerned about losing their credibility as a result of speaking up and often expressed this as a concern about being labeled as a trouble-maker or "not a team player." People sense that this repercussion has a long-term impact on employment and relationships at work.

■ Failing to speak up has a negative impact on both the person and the organization, including loss of pro-

---

1. Kathleen D. Ryan and Daniel K. Oestreich, *Driving Fear Out of the Workplace: How to Overcome the Invisible Barriers to Quality, Productivity, and Innovation* (San Francisco: Jossey-Bass, 1991).

ductivity, an increased likelihood of making errors, negative attitudes toward the organization, failure to meet deadlines or budgets, and loss of self-esteem.

The commitment behind our work is to help our clients build workplaces that are characterized by trust and collaboration. We know that the destructive patterns described above are not inevitable. When they do exist, we know that they can be turned around. An important piece of that turnaround is what people personally decide to do. When faced with potential repercussions, will they choose to say what they think?

Driving Fear Out of the Workplace made the point that leaders must take the initiative to create safe work environments, free from blame and repercussions. But leaders cannot do this alone. Their partners in this effort must be individuals who are willing to push past their hesitation in order to become courageous messengers. A primary view held throughout this book is that it is everyone's job to help the news to get through.

How This Book Is Organized

Each part of this book is framed with some aspect of courage and is generally structured around the cycle of speaking up. This cycle begins at the point where a person senses the need to say something but hesitates to do so. It continues through an actual conversation about the message to a point of reflection about the experience. This is graphically represented in Figure 1.1, which indicates what chapters will be useful to you at key points along your way. We also present written descriptions of each of the book's parts.

Part One, "Everyday Acts of Courage," introduces the structure of the book and the definitions and principles that form the foundation of the text.

Part Two, "Finding the Courage," is a guided reflection that will enable readers to discover their message and motivation

for speaking up, the risks involved, and other reasons why they

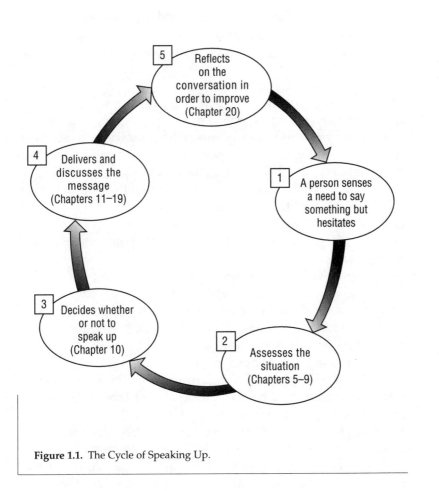

Figure 1.1. The Cycle of Speaking Up.

may hesitate. Chapter Ten, which ends this part, asks whether the messenger is going to speak up or not and provides support for whatever choice is made.

Part Three, "Acting with Courage," presents the nuts and bolts of delivering a message. Messengers are advised about each phase of the conversation with a receiver: getting ready for and opening the conversation, presenting the message, talking things through, wrapping up, and following through. Concrete do's and don'ts are found throughout.

Part Four, "The Tough Cases," addresses some of the most difficult situations that messengers face. The advice builds on the six steps outlined in Part Three, with tips on how to navigate more complex and risky situations.

Part Five, "Sustaining the Courage," focuses on the larger meaning of speaking up. This part emphasizes the importance of reflecting on and learning from a messenger experience. The personal transformation that occurs when individuals act with courage and integrity is explored. A final chapter is devoted to the belief that skilled and courageous messengers have an enormous ability to make positive changes within their organization.

Several additional resources are grouped in the Messenger's Tool Box. Here you will find: a set of exercises for learning and personal development keyed to each chapter, an overview of basic interpersonal communication skills, and advice about how to receive a difficult message from someone else. For readers operating in an on-line or dispersed work site environment, thoughts are presented on how to deliver a message when a face-to-face meeting is not possible. A summary listing of all the book's tips on effectively bringing forward and discussing the message is available for quick review.

The cycle reflected in Figure 1.1 is important to keep in mind as you read and refer to the book over time. As situations arise, you may find yourself going back and working through some or all of the parts. For example, say that you "found the courage" in one situation and delivered a successful message. You may realize that you want to review that same material again given other, more demanding circumstances. You may come to see the cycle as we do—a continuous, outward spiral leading to increasing levels of confidence and skill. This repetitive aspect is what eventually leads to the personal transformation explored in the last part of the book.

 PERSONAL EXERCISES

General Exercise 1.1. Your Reasons for Reading This Book

General Exercise 1.2. Responsibilities of Leaders and Messengers

2

COURAGEOUS MESSENGERS

THROUGHOUT THIS BOOK, you will meet more than a dozen courageous messengers. Their experiences reinforce the very human aspects of what courageous messengers face as they bring forward their tough news. Their stories provide real-world reference points to help you to explore your own feelings, knowledge, skills, and experiences.

Making Courage Real

Sarah Eastland is a courageous messenger who spoke up to her peer group, her company's president, and her vice president. She witnessed the gradual breakdown of leadership and communication above and around her. The high level of mistrust that resulted took an increasing toll on Sarah, her work, and her workplace relationships. Although she was very aware of the risks she faced, Sarah spoke up because she cared about the future success of her organization. She did so many times and with a consistent message.

Hers is a complex story, and one that could be described as a tough case. Yet it contains three themes that are a part of the less dramatic, everyday experiences of most workplace messengers. They are the *Three R's:*

1. People want workplace *relationships* in which they feel free to speak up.

2. Speaking up requires courage because *risks* are present.

3. Speaking up can have *rewards* for the messenger and the organization.

As you read about Sarah and her speaking-up experiences, look for the way the Three R's play themselves out. Pay attention to the way these dynamics remind you of past or current experiences of your own. Think about Sarah, the circumstances she faced, and the personal characteristics she demonstrated. To what degree do you see qualities of yourself reflected in her courage and commitment?

Sarah's Story: "We Need Help"

Sarah was a manager in the home office of a large, well-respected insurance company, which was recognized as being among the top companies nationally. Jobs such as hers were envied. Turnover was low because people tended to stay and hoped to move up within the company. Sarah reported to one of two associate vice presidents who reported to Dave Trimbull, a senior vice president. Dave had been hired from outside the company less than six months prior to the beginning of this story.

Dave's honeymoon period was definitely over. Difficulties existed between him and his associate vice presidents (AVPs). His style was quite different from that of his predecessor. He had made some changes that others did not like. The AVPs resented the fact that Dave had come from outside the company and had taken one of the few senior positions left. The AVPs were subtly saying things to the line managers that discredited Dave's leadership. And so the discord at the top of the division spread to the manager group. Cliques had formed, centering around their position for or against the AVPs and Dave. Those who did not take sides remained quiet, feeling caught between Dave, his direct reports, and several of their peers who were resisting Dave's leadership.

Sarah remembers that "every meeting, whether it was with the manager group or with the AVPs, was consumed by the relationship and trust issues. There wasn't any focus on our business, on any of the changes that were beginning to affect us in the industry. All we ended up talking about was the situation." Miscommunication flourished. Cooperative decision making among the managers was almost impossible. Sarah had been in her manager's job for only a year. She describes herself at that time as being competent, "but I still needed coaching to be effective. I had disengaged from my peers and my AVP because I disagreed with just sitting around in a room griping. That meant that I really didn't have anyone I could go to for advice."

The continuing negativity and her inability to do her best work finally got to Sarah. In spite of the risk of being labeled by her peers, she started challenging members of the group. She would say things like "This isn't being constructive. This constant complaining won't change anything. We can't just stay stuck." Members would respond to her by saying, "Well, you can't expect us to say anything. It's too risky." Sarah kept repeating her message because she knew that she could not stay in an environment that was so negative. She did not want to leave her job or the company. Finally, as a group, the managers agreed to schedule a meeting with the president to discuss their concerns about Dave—but only if Sarah acted as the spokesperson.

At this meeting, the president listened to the group's message, delivered by Sarah. "We said we didn't have confidence in our senior vice president, that things were going on between him and the AVPs. That nothing was working for us." The president listened carefully, then reacted strongly—but not in the way they had hoped. Angrily, he sent them back with instructions to deal with this themselves, to be responsible leaders, to take constructive action rather than acting like children. Sarah's first reaction was: "Oh, no, what have we done? What's going to happen now?" Yet she knew in her heart that the president was right. The next day, Sarah took action. She went to see Dave.

Going into the meetings with the president and Dave, Sarah was very aware of the risk she was taking. "Throughout all of this, the only reprisal I ever worried about had to do with damaging my credibility. That is very important to me." Yet Sarah knew that the risk of not speaking up was far greater than that of saying what was on her mind. "I had never done anything like this before—complaining about people above me in the organization. But watching my peer group disintegrate was even worse than having my bosses be mad at me. I was willing to do all this because things were going nowhere and getting more and more negative. It was hard to see a talented group go down because they didn't know how to handle a problem." Even so, walking into Dave's office, Sarah worried that he would think badly of her, that nothing would change, that all of the negativity would continue.

Dave's response to Sarah's message was unexpected. "I told him that things were not going well. That his conflict with the AVPs was causing major problems for the managers, who were trying to keep product development going. We needed to do something about this and do it soon! I suggested that we needed to figure out how to work together and to sort out what was going on. I also said that to get back on track, we needed some outside help." Dave agreed with Sarah and surprised her by requesting that she immediately brainstorm with him about what could be done and the help they would need to move forward. After the fact, Sarah recognized that Dave "must have been in a lot of pain about what was going on. He was very open to what I had to say."

Over the next year, people throughout the division began to work on a variety of issues under the guidance of a steering committee, with help from a consultant. The steering committee included Dave, an AVP, Sarah, and three other managers. They concentrated on the underlying issues of mistrust,

12

messy communication, confusion in roles, and ineffective decision making. It was hard work facing up to these issues, much less knowing what to do about them. The committee was successful in defining a team development effort for the division as a whole. As a result of everyone's efforts, things improved dramatically over the course of the next two years. Both Sarah and Dave stayed with the company. In fact, they are still in the same organization and are very successful.

Some years later, when he was asked about his perspective on the story, Dave echoed many of the same points that Sarah had told us. Unknown to Sarah was the resignation that Dave had been ready to submit to the president. Without any visible signs of support from his staff, Dave had given up hope that he could turn things around without major trauma to the productivity of the division. When Sarah brought him her message and a suggestion about what to do, Dave saw that he was not completely isolated from his staff. He was more than ready to give it a try.

Dave recalls that if someone had not taken the action that Sarah did, "there would have been a bloodbath. As it turned out, I had strong support from the president, so I would have retained my position. But a number of others would have had to leave. Through sheer guts I probably would have been able to build some level of trust, but it never really would have worked. I would have ended up being the slash-and-burn change agent, cleaning up the most pressing problems. But then I would have had to leave too. And somebody else would have been hired to put it together, to help people come together and rebuild productivity."

When each of them is asked about the benefits that resulted from Sarah's message and Dave's response, their answers are quite similar. For Dave, the immediate crisis was resolved. The long-term development of his operating area began. He was able to stay with the company, fulfilling his potential as a skilled and effective leader. For Sarah, the situation and her relationship with her peers improved. The division's development effort opened up great opportunities for her personal and professional growth. Both Sarah and Dave recognize that their conversation began a unique and powerful working relationship that continues today. In Chapter Twenty-One, we will return to their story.

The Three R's of Speaking Up

Sarah's story illustrates the Three R's—themes that almost always emerge when people share their stories about speaking up. Although the details of their stories may differ, the Three R's are consistently a part of people's experiences.

People Want Workplace Relationships in Which They Feel Free to Speak Up

Speaking up almost always takes place within an ongoing work relationship. That is why it should not be thought of as a one-time event. Rather, it is an opportunity to contribute to the development of a continuing relationship. In the best of circumstances, both the messenger and the receiver are skilled communicators and are committed to building productive, trust-based relationships.

In such cases, the open exchange of even the most difficult news can be a source of learning, mutual influence, and personal connection. People feel free of the threat of blame and intimidation. This is the kind of relationship people want at work—a relationship that is open, honest, and caring; that can handle clear, direct discussions of sensitive subjects; where intentions are assumed to be honorable; and where differences are appreciated and seen as a source of strength.

Sarah recognized that she could not continue to work in an environment where relationships were based on mistrust and suspicion. She was willing to take risks because she wanted working relationships that were positive, creative, and supportive. She spoke up to her peers, her president, and her vice president, even though she hoped to have continuing relationships with all of them. Because these relationships were ongoing, the risks she faced were keenly felt.

Speaking Up Requires Courage Because Risks Are Present

When a person hesitates to speak up and asks, even for an instant, "Is this such a good idea?" or "Should I go ahead with this?" it is an indication that risk is present. Courage enables a person to take the risk—to step into the unknown, take a chance, or, if need be, face the consequences.

The risks reflect possible repercussions. These can consist of either short- or longer-term negative effects on the messenger's employment situation or working relationships. If a messenger has suffered repercussions in the past or has been close to a situation where someone has paid a price for speaking up, these fears are even more likely to be present. As with Sarah, the fear most people have is that their reputation or credibility will be damaged. They worry that being labeled a troublemaker, a whiner, or "not a team player" will lead to other repercussions, such as:

- Getting assigned to a worse job or a worse shift
- Being cut out of the information loop
- Losing others' respect as a person or as a contributor
- Receiving a poor performance review
- Being ostracized by their peers
- Ending up on a layoff list
- Being fired

Messengers of tough news often play in a world of personal high stakes, even if the message itself is not world-shaking. Although Sarah's story is more dramatic than most, many of the stories in the coming pages can be described as "everyday." Even so, to the messenger in the moment, these situations can be very serious—especially when they are cast in the light of possible long-term repercussions.

Speaking Up Can Have Rewards for the Messenger and the Organization

Two primary rewards come from speaking up: *positive change* and *a sense of integrity*. Often, as in Sarah's case, these two are connected. Changes are *not* possible if people do not speak up. If people cannot raise their concerns, observations, or ideas, problems will not be identified and solved. Think of the following familiar situations:

- Customers leave in frustration over small details of service.

- Budgets become devoted to the wrong priorities or political game playing.

- People spend too much time correcting errors or engaging in rework.

- Someone's personal style keeps a team in a constant state of frustration.

Where issues such as these have become undiscussable because of the risks associated with speaking up, improvements cannot be made.

Sarah experienced the best reward for a messenger. She saw change happening when the conflicts between Dave and the AVPs were addressed and when her peer group stopped the constant gossip and negativity. She recognized her influence in getting the problems corrected. From the beginning, Sarah knew that she was speaking up because her values told her that it was the right thing to do. The progress achieved over time by her co-workers was a confirmation not only of her skills and positive impact, but of these basic values as well.

As you will see from other stories, not every message situation results in a major workplace improvement or a change in someone's behavior. When this doesn't happen, most messengers at least find quiet satisfaction in knowing that they "did the right thing." When people operate in this way, speaking up is typically "worth it" regardless of the actual results.

The Three R's are like three ways of seeing the same box. From one angle, being a messenger is about creating effective relationships at work. From another, it is about the risks, real or imagined, that must be faced. And from a third viewpoint, it is about the rewards, for the person and for the organization. These different perspectives tumble through the stories ahead. As you see their influence in the pages to come, turn the box over in your mind, viewing the messenger's experience from each of these angles.

Successfully Speaking Up About Tough Issues

Organizations can no longer afford to maintain a work environment where people do not identify problems or offer ideas for improvements. More than ever before, to survive and succeed, organizations need people to speak up. The capacity to be the messenger, to say the hard things that need to be said, is at the heart of what we see as the transformation of the workplace. These changes are clearly connected to global economic and social shifts. Yet we know that they are played out daily, in highly personal situations, as individuals like Sarah Eastland decide, "I'm going to say something about this one. It's worth it."

Our objective with this book is to help you to be more successful when you decide that an issue is worth the risk. We offer a conscious process you can use to prepare for and carry out your role as a messenger. And after you have spoken up, we want you, like Sarah, to be able to answer the following four questions with an enthusiastic "Yes!"

1. Did I do the right thing?

2. Did I do it well?

3. Was it well received?

4. Did it result in positive change?

If you can do this, you will have had the experience of being a successful messenger. We have written this book to help you to have this experience.

PERSONAL
EXERCISE

General Exercise 2.1. Your Experience with the Three R's

3

MESSENGERS AND TOUGH NEWS

S PEAKING UP NEEDS TO be an *everyday* act of courage, not an extraordinary event. But because our working worlds are complex, the messages that need to be sent are often complex, too. People are caught between the desire to speak up regularly and the fact that messengers must work with sensitive news and complicated situations.

This chapter is designed to help you get a handle on some of this complexity by exploring exactly what messages are about. There are three basic categories of content. A single message may be about one, two, or all three of these areas. This breakdown can help you to think more clearly about the content of your own messages and why they sometimes feel very difficult to send. As you read the following three stories, see if you can determine the nature of these content areas.

 Shawna's Story:
"The Wrong Candidate for the Job"

Shawna dropped by Carmen's office after everyone else had left the building. Sure enough, Carmen, head of the division, was there. Shawna was an administrative specialist and Carmen was the person who had hired her four years ago prior to being promoted to division director. Theirs continued to be an easy working relationship, one that Shawna valued immensely. She knew that Carmen respected both her work and her opinions. After Carmen had been promoted, Shawna had purposely kept a bit of distance between them. She didn't want her co-workers to think that she had a special "in" with the director. And yet, in a way, that was true.

Shawna was concerned about who would fill the manager's job that Carmen had left when she was promoted. Since Shawna was a member of the committee that had just finished interviewing candidates for the position, it was fairly simple to slide into a conversation in which she asked Carmen for her thoughts about the candidates. That was when she learned that Bob, the acting manager in the position for the last six months, was probably Carmen's choice. "After all," Carmen had said, "he's been with the organization a long time and as far as I know, he probably deserves a promotion. What do you think?" These were the words that rolled over and over in Shawna's head as she made her way home from work that evening, tying her stomach in knots.

Stunned and disappointed at what she had heard, she had avoided answering Carmen's "What do you think?" question. Having reported to Bob directly for the last six months, Shawna knew exactly what she thought about him, but she needed time to decide if she should say anything to Carmen.

On more than one occasion, Shawna had found herself thinking, "*Acting* manager is right. This guy couldn't manage his way out of a paper bag!" She had spent several months watching him give vague assignments, change his mind, not follow through, and ignore the obvious violations of the sick leave and overtime policies of one of his favorites. He was avoiding his responsibilities and Shawna took the brunt. She answered his E-mail and made decisions about who would be at his meetings and what the agenda ought to be. She had little respect for him and believed that it would be a serious mistake for the organization if he were to be placed permanently in the manager's job. If he got the job, she knew that she would not be able to work for him.

Many questions and concerns swirled about her. If she decided to share her concerns with Carmen, what was the best, most professional way to do it? If she told Carmen about some of what she had experienced in the last six months, would it be an inappropriate sharing of confidential information? What were the ethics involved in a situation that could well cost Bob this promotion? Shawna worried that if the word got out about what she had done, it might permanently damage her relationship with Bob and with her co-workers as well. Was she simply being selfish and immature about this whole thing because she did not like working for him? Yet in the midst of this self-questioning, Shawna could not escape a sense of dread every time she thought of Bob managing a department of sixty people.

Shawna decided that she needed to share her concerns with Carmen. In a meeting with her the next day, Shawna summarized her thoughts: "The bottom line is that I feel Bob will be a weak manager. From what I've seen so far, he is not well organized, is poor on follow-through, and uses some questionable management practices. I hope you'll look further into this before you make your decision."

Carmen paid attention to what Shawna had to say about Bob. Shortly after Shawna expressed her concerns, Carmen heard other complaints about him. She began an investigation into some of his management practices, including possible favoritism related to overtime and sick leave violations. Bob did not get the promotion to the manager's job.

Bernice's Story:
"A Shade of Florence"

"I'm not sure what's going on here, but this really makes me nervous," thought Bernice, as she waited, hoping that Louise was at home and that she would pick up the phone. On the fifth ring, the melodic voice that Bernice had learned *not* to trust answered with a warm "This is Louise."

Bernice, a twenty-four-year-old nurse manager, took a deep breath and explained the potentially serious situation at the hospital: the weekend shift was forty-five minutes from beginning and the nursing floor was full of patients, including two intensive-care patients who had lidocaine drips with pumps that needed monitoring according to specific hospital procedures. For some reason, half of the regular staff had called in sick; Bernice was the only registered nurse available to work with the one licensed practical nurse and three nursing assistants who had come to work. She had exhausted all the normal sources for additional staff; none were available in the area. Knowing that there was no way that she and the others could adequately care for their patients, Bernice was calling Louise, the nursing administrator, to ask for assistance—or at least for permission to transfer some of the less acute patients to another hospital fifteen miles away.

When Bernice finished her summary, there was silence. Finally, Louise spoke. "Really, Bernice, I think you are making too big a deal out of this. You're just a year out of that hot-shot university program. Why don't you put some of that higher education to work and take care of this situation yourself?" Somehow, Bernice and the weekend staff survived, but at a risk to the safety of the patients.

On Monday, when she checked in with some of her co-workers, Bernice heard the phrase that would come to represent the price of her call to Louise: "Bernice? She's merely a shade of Florence Nightingale, that's all she is—unable to persevere when it gets tough. Not exactly a credit to our profession, is she?" Speaking in a confidential tone to a few key people on staff, Louise made it clear that her reputation for retaliating against those she decided were "complainers" was well deserved. It didn't take long for the "shade of Florence" story to circulate through the hospital.

It didn't matter that the circumstances Bernice was forced to contend with over the weekend went against everything she had learned in school and the standards of patient care she was committed to protect. It didn't matter that Louise had a reputation for unfair retaliation and Bernice was young and new to her career. What mattered was that Bernice interrupted Louise's weekend with a problem that she "should have solved on her own." From Louise's point of view, such behavior was not to be tolerated and the sooner Bernice learned her lesson, the better it would be for everyone involved.

As a result of this and other experiences, Bernice decided to leave the organization. She was deeply offended by Louise's retaliation and her disregard for patient safety. She knew that she had been labeled as a troublemaker and that her relationship with Louise was irreparably damaged because of it. Staying in the organization didn't make sense. Louise's actions taught Bernice a lot about what *not* to do as a leader, a lesson that served her well as her career progressed. In the near term, the incident inspired Bernice to go back to school so that in the future she would have greater opportunities to influence the way care was delivered to patients.

Chris's Story: "But Jamal Thinks Everything Is Fine"

Finally, with a tone of exasperation, Chris's wife, Phyllis, said, "Honey, when are you going to talk to Jamal? This has been going on too long. It's driving you crazy and, frankly, I'm getting tired of listening to it." She was right, of course. Chris knew that the time had come to let Jamal know that his absences as manager of the unit were creating a major problem. Chris had hesitated because he didn't want to hurt Jamal's feelings. Managers like him didn't come along every day. He was more than a boss—he was a friend, too.

Chris worked in a small staff unit of a large manufacturing plant in the Southeast. Jamal, as the manager, was a pivotal member of the team. For the environment and type of work they were doing, Jamal's style was unusual— nondirective, open-minded, always assuming the best about people, a team member even though he was in charge. The problem was that over the last year or so, Jamal's job had greatly expanded. This meant that he was gone more and more as he concentrated on corporate rather than work group issues. When he was around, it was always so busy that he really never had the chance to see how dysfunctional things had become.

When Jamal was gone, Chris could see major communication problems emerge among the staff and with some of the other internal service

23

departments in the factory. Resource issues were left hanging. People didn't follow through on their commitments. Many of the maintenance tasks were not being taken care of because staff members goofed off when things were slow. Because everyone reported directly to Jamal and because they all had an image of being part of a "happy family," no one would jump in to hold others accountable for their behavior when Jamal was not around. It had gotten to the point where Chris could not do the kind of quality work he was personally committed to. In addition, he was becoming increasingly uncomfortable with his own dishonesty. Not addressing the problems, pretending that everything was fine when it wasn't, made Chris feel as if he was living a lie.

Chris was well aware of the risks. He had thought about them a lot. First, this sort of feedback was not something he had ever given a supervisor before. If Jamal got angry when he heard what was going on, everyone on the staff could be negatively affected. If Jamal did nothing as a result of the feedback, then Chris's credibility would be diminished. If Jamal took the feedback personally, it might deflate his own level of confidence in his ability to lead. And there was always the risk that any of these possible responses might damage the personal and professional relationship Chris truly enjoyed with Jamal. As he imagined having the conversation with Jamal, Chris could not predict how Jamal might respond to the information that had to be shared.

Chris took Jamal to lunch and outlined his concerns. Jamal was shocked. He'd had no idea that the situation had gotten so out of hand. He thanked Chris for his willingness to give him the feedback, asked to have the notes that Chris had brought along, and said that he needed time to think it all over. Within a week, Jamal brought everyone together for discussions that led to a reorganization of the unit. The new structure preserved the spirit of teamwork but added some clear decision-making roles so that the daily operations did not depend on Jamal's being present.

What Messengers Speak Up About

Messengers like Shawna, Bernice, and Chris speak up to improve things at work. They make a request for action based on information, opinions, data, or observations, some of which may be threatening to their receivers. For example, Shawna's comments might have threatened Carmen by questioning her judgment of Bob. Bernice challenged Louise with a high-risk situation that required an immediate decision. Chris's feedback might have embarrassed Jamal by bringing to light problems with the management of his work group.

It is worth remembering that people also bring forward positive and nonthreatening news. Although it is important to discuss these issues, people worry much less about how to present something that is viewed as good news. This is why, in this book, the focus is on the messages that are characterized as:

- Tough issues

- Difficult subjects

- Sensitive topics

- Bad news

Keep in mind that what is "bad news" for one person could be an exciting opportunity for another. A new idea may be difficult for one individual and a boon to the next. Whatever these subjective responses may be, the content of tough messages tends to fall into one of three categories: work outcomes, working relationships, or personal behavior. Look closely at the three stories and you will see that the content of each messenger's news reflects the overlapping nature of these categories. Figure 3.1 graphically displays this interaction.

These dynamic and interconnected areas can be more fully defined in the following ways:

WORK OUTCOMES

- What work is accomplished

- How the work is organized

- The quality or amount of work that gets done

- Customer satisfaction

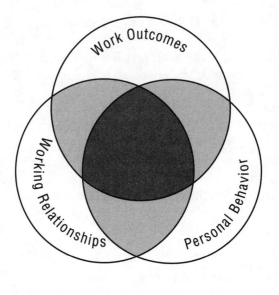

Figure 3.1. What Messages Are About.

WORKING RELATIONSHIPS

- How two or more people work together
- The feelings they have toward one another
- How a person feels about the organization
- How a person feels treated by the organization
- How the interaction causes someone to feel about himself or herself

PERSONAL BEHAVIOR

- A person's performance of job responsibilities
- Other aspects of a person's behavior that go on in the work environment
- The style or attitudes that shape the way a person behaves in the workplace

Complex, Overlapping Concerns

Frequently the initial concern of the messenger is in one area, but it has implications for another. The message is larger than it first might seem. A straightforward illustration of this is Shawna's story. Her message to Carmen is about Bob's personal behavior—his performance as an acting manager. But her message really incorporates issues of working relationships in her office as well as work outcomes. Without directly commenting on relationships or outcomes, she has given Carmen a message in all three areas.

In Bernice's case, the focus of the message is on work outcomes. Although it is easy to see that she is worried about some of Louise's behavior and their relationship, these points are not talked about. They are a backdrop to the presented message, which is simply about work outcomes.

Finally, Chris's message seems to be primarily about the working relationships in the office and work outcomes. But it also directly relates to Jamal's personal behavior: he should have known about the problems, even if his absences were inevitable. So Chris's message, like Shawna's, involves all three content areas.

Complex messages are not necessarily more threatening to address. What counts is whether the messenger and receiver can talk easily about any of the areas related to the message. If not, it becomes more difficult to send the message because of the sense of threat that comes from points that cannot be openly and directly discussed.

Because the workplace is about work—and getting work done—addressing work-related outcomes may be the least difficult and most significant starting point for a tough news conversation. When personal behavior and working relationships also need to be brought in, a skilled messenger will be able to present them in the context of work outcomes. In many cases, this makes them more understandable and less threatening to discuss.

In the chapters that follow, notice they way overlapping concerns are interwoven into core messages. The more skillful a messenger is in talking about any of the three areas—personal behavior, working relationships, and work outcomes—the more likely it is that a complex message will be understood correctly and acted upon appropriately by the receiver.

 PERSONAL EXERCISES

Story Exercise 3.1. Challenges Faced by Shawna, Bernice, and Chris

General Exercise 3.2. What Type of Messages Do *You* Send?

4

BECOMING
A SKILLED
MESSENGER

G IVEN THE RISK THAT
can be associated
with being a mes-
senger, it makes sense to evaluate how a
person might increase his or her chance
for success. Let's begin by drawing a distinction between a skilled messenger and
a successful one. A skilled messenger is
someone who can bring up a difficult
subject in a manner that is:

- Clear

- Direct

- Sincere

- Constructive

This skilled individual *presents the message so that the receiver hears and understands what is being said.* A successful messenger, by comparison, is someone who, after having delivered the news, *gets the desired outcomes or some other satisfying solution.* A skilled messenger is not necessarily a successful one. This is an uncomfortable distinction, because it really means that even the most able messenger may not get what she or he wants. When messengers consciously work on their skills and approach, they significantly improve their chances of achieving success.

This chapter highlights some guiding principles on which you can build your messenger skills. Once they are in place, they become the keys that will help to unlock your success as a messenger. Keep in mind that certain aspects of a speaking-up situation make it easier to be successful, no matter what the messenger brings by way of understanding and capability. For example, it will be easier if:

- The receiver is receptive to hearing tough news

- The messenger has a naturally confident interpersonal style

- The messenger has had positive experiences speaking up in the past

- The organization supports people taking such risks

But whether or not these dynamics are present, the principles form a foundation for your skills and can make a significant difference. These fundamentals cross virtually all messenger situations. As a way to get into them, consider the case of Ted.

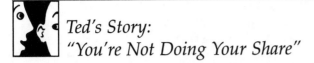

Ted's Story: "You're Not Doing Your Share"

Ted works in the shipping department for a small-parts manufacturing plant. At the time of this story, four people worked in the shipping department, including Marge, a truck driver for the company. The size of the department meant that everyone had to help out to get the work done. When she was not out on a delivery, Marge was expected to pitch in with parts picking and counting, packing, loading, and cleanup. Their biggest customer used a just-in-time inventory system, so the shipping department was always under a lot of pressure to perform.

Each day Ted watched Marge come back from a delivery and, as often as not, go to the break room and sit there until another delivery was scheduled. When someone would say something to her, Marge might get up and help. But it was just as likely that she would snap and growl until the person backed off. At over six feet and 230 pounds, she made others reluctant to mess with her.

Everyone complained about Marge behind her back, but no one would confront her, not only because of her intimidating demeanor but also because her father worked for the company and was well liked and respected by everyone. No one wanted to get on the wrong side of Marge's dad. People suspected that her mood had something to do with her home life, but they did not want to ask about it. It was obvious that behind her grouchiness, she was struggling with something private and meant to keep her distance. As Ted said, "This was one of those situations where you just didn't know how the person—Marge or her dad—was going to respond."

After three months of scrambling to keep up with the demand on the dock, Ted had had enough. His first attempt at some type of action was to try to get Zack, the lead worker, to confront Marge. Ted talked to Zack several times, but Zack made it clear that he did not want to take this one on. He had just been appointed to the lead role and was not up to confronting anyone, much less Marge. Going to supervisors higher in the company was not an option either. That would be breaking the code and would be seen as ratting on a fellow union member. The only options remaining for Ted were to say something to Marge or stay silent. He decided that he had to do the right thing, by getting direct and to the point.

Ted spoke to Marge when everyone was present one morning: "I don't know what your problem is, Marge, but whatever it is, you're not pulling your part of the load around here. Your moods and lack of help are driving the rest of us nuts. We can't keep up with the pace without your help. You need to get to work when you're here in the plant. It's not a fair deal when we bust our butts and you sit. We need your help."

When she found herself confronted so directly, Marge dropped her jaw and sat looking stunned for several moments. She didn't say a thing but her eyes grew large. Finally, she grabbed her clipboard, went to her truck, and drove away. She didn't return until late afternoon. She didn't say anything to anybody about what had happened that morning, but it was obvious that she was in a different, better mood. She pitched right in with some of the end-of-day cleanup work.

The next day and in the days following, things clearly were different. Marge worked as hard as anyone and her snarling attitude was much less in evidence. Ted never found out what had been bothering her, but life in the shipping department definitely improved.

Guiding Principles for Skillful Messengers

Ted's story represents a jumping-off point for exploring most of the principles that guide skilled and successful messengers. Consider this an overview of what will be covered in more depth in the chapters ahead.

Skilled messengers reflect on their decision to speak up. The best way to develop the personal strength and courage to play the messenger's role is to spend focused time reflecting on the situation. Preparation, even if it is momentary, helps messengers to express their views more effectively. They are *choosing* to speak up—it is not a careless outburst. Ted went through a period of self-reflection. He considered the risks and rewards of speaking up. He reflected on his relationships with his fellow union members, Marge, Marge's dad, and his co-workers as he tried to decide what to do. After careful consideration, he decided that his motivations—getting the job done and fairness—outweighed the possible risks.

Skilled messengers think about their strategies for communicating. Messengers consider in advance what they want to say and how to say it. They do this in order to have the maximum possible chance of being successful. Strategy means asking, "How can I express myself in an honest way so that the receiver will understand?" Rehearsing the words, choosing a time and place for a conversation, thinking about the likely effects on others—all of these things are the messenger's strategic concerns. Although Ted's interaction with Marge might be seen by some as not very elegant, it was simple, clean, and to the point. He deliberately chose to speak in front of the whole crew so that it would be clear that the others also felt the same way.

Skilled messengers are clear and assertive, not belligerent or abrasive. Many people have an uncomfortable image of speaking up, believing that it usually leads to some kind of confrontational exchange. Ted was certainly direct and assertive, but he was not angry or hostile. When receivers feel attacked because the messenger is belligerent, they become understandably defensive. In such cases they are not likely to listen carefully to the message being discussed. Ted did not attack Marge's character or question her work ethic. He simply stated what he saw and what he needed from her.

Clear personal values often shape a message. Ted's message was not just about ending nonproductive behavior; it was also about doing what was right for his workplace and his team. His motives contained no ambiguity. He had nothing to gain politically from intervening. His motivation was to create an environment where work was fairly distributed. The messenger's values not only make it easier to speak up; they also serve as motivation and help the receiver to know what the messenger's motives are.

Speaking up is often more than a single conversation. Although Ted was successful with Marge by using one direct statement, this is not always the case. Often, speaking up involves several conversations with the receiver or others. Keep in mind that Ted felt that Zack, the lead worker, was the best person to deliver the message. If he had stopped his efforts when Zack refused to help, the changes that resulted would never have been realized.

Messengers who think of their work as consisting of a single try may not fully demonstrate the depth of their convictions or enable the message eventually to be heard.

Skilled messengers see face-to-face conversation as important but are open to other means of communication. In the vast majority of situations, the messenger and receiver meet to discuss the problem, idea, or concern together. But other forms of communication also can come into play. Sometimes engaging someone else to present your message can be very helpful. This is particularly true in situations where gender, racial, cultural, or hierarchical differences create tension and mistrust between the receiver and the messenger. In some circumstances, the use of E-mail or an old-fashioned written note can open the door for a later conversation. Effective messengers use methods that convey awareness of the receiver's circumstances as a way to set the stage for the conversation.

Skilled messengers consciously apply interpersonal communication skills. When the issues are complex, the capacity to sort things out becomes crucial. Well-developed interpersonal skills enable the messenger to ask effective questions, pull out hidden assumptions about a situation, respond to the feeling tone of the conversation, and tactfully express a point. In the Messenger's Tool Box and throughout this book, you will find material devoted to these skills.

A Foundation

Over the years we have developed a set of phrases, or *affirmations*, that provide support and guidance for us when we are in the messenger role. They help us to structure a positive and courageous approach, both when preparing for and when discussing a message. In a way, they can be considered the foundation for the principles we have outlined above. You may want to adopt the ones listed here or develop your own:

"I'm here to build a collaborative relationship, not to be right."

"I'm here to identify and solve a problem, not to place blame."

"I can influence the outcome of this conversation, but I cannot control it."

"I am willing to do the hard work necessary to create understanding."

"I will share all relevant information with integrity."

"I am clear about what I am trying to accomplish."

"I trust myself to be okay, regardless of how this turns out."

As you can see, these are simple statements that get straight to the point and come directly from the heart. They fit tightly together to shape a powerful value base that is very much a part of the courage necessary to move ahead.

 PERSONAL EXERCISES

General Exercise 4.1. Your Observations About Skilled Messengers

General Exercise 4.2. Your Own Affirmations

General Exercise 4.3. Restating Affirmations as Behaviors

PART II

FINDING THE COURAGE

5

COURAGE IS AN INSIDE JOB

INDING THE COURAGE to speak up is an inside job. Courageous messengers look directly at the situations they face in light of what they think, what they feel, and how they respond to risky or fearful situations. Courage is gained by directly facing the fears or other factors that block open communication about difficult issues. By approaching these barriers in steps, messengers gain insight about themselves and their situations. As they do so, their fears recede and are replaced by the courage to speak up.

This pattern is similar to the recent adventure of a friend who decided to go on a vision quest. To complete this experience, he would spend three days and nights in the desert by himself. Before the experience, he worried about all manner of mishaps and fearful possibilities. His guides asked him to face up to these worries in advance, to talk about them, and to evaluate them. The process of getting ready for his time alone caused him to reflect deeply. When the time came to begin his quest, he found that he had the courage needed to hike alone far from the base camp. Afterward, he told us how powerful his experience had been and how much more confident he felt in taking charge of his career and life.

Finding your courage to speak up starts well before your message is ever delivered, just as our friend's quest really began long before he reached the desert. Five steps can help you get ready for your journey as a messenger. Figure 5.1 is a visual representation of this process:

1. *Know your true message:* What do you really want to say?

2. *Know your real motivation:* Why are you bringing this message forward?

3. *Assess your risks:* What repercussions might happen if you speak up?

4. *Understand your "yes-buts":* What other reasons cause you to hesitate?

5. *Make a decision:* Are you going to speak up?

You can see how the decision to speak up is determined by how you balance the importance of your message and motivation against the power of the risks and yes-buts. A chapter is devoted to each of these steps. Working through them, in order, will:

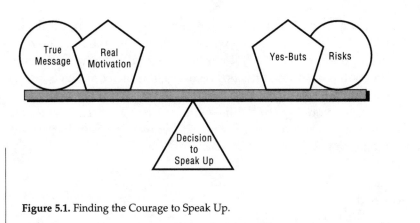

Figure 5.1. Finding the Courage to Speak Up.

■ Increase your clarity about what you want to say, why you want to say it, and the reasons you find yourself hesitating to do so

■ Enable you to gradually and thoughtfully approach the decision of whether to speak up or not

■ Increase your confidence if you do decide to go ahead

Slowing down to do this internal reflection can sometimes be the hardest part of speaking up, especially if you are a person who likes to get straight to the action. If the exploration reveals some uncomfortable insights about past patterns of behavior or emotions, you may find it particularly challenging. But as with the case of our friend and his desert quest, taking the time to fully prepare for the decision to speak up can yield exceptional benefits later on.

Mastering these steps will enable you to easily evaluate a range of possible speaking-up situations. Although the process is thorough, over time you will find yourself quickly applying principles rather than following a series of consciously considered steps. If you go ahead, you will be better positioned for a successful speaking-up experience. If you decide not to speak up, you will possess the confidence that comes from having carefully explored the situation you face. "Now is not the time" is a wise decision when it is reached in a conscious and thoughtful manner. But if you back away without examining the internal questions posed in the next five chapters, regardless of your decision, you will have missed the opportunity to more completely understand yourself.

As you step up to this inside journey, first read the following story. It will be used throughout the chapters in Part Two to illustrate key points.

 Terri's Story:
"A Hard Time with Conflict"

"How much worse is this going to get?" Terri asked herself. She had just finished reading the memo that Richard, her boss, had sent out to her department outlining a change of assignments. It was announced that Terri's role had shifted and that Enrique would now be working with Nellis on the manufacturing audit. "I never thought that those conversations with him about the problems with Nellis would result in this!" she thought. "I guess he must think I'm completely incompetent." Sick at heart and wondering what the future would hold, Terri grabbed her purse and left work for the day.

Six months ago, it was a different story. At the age of thirty-one, Terri had been identified as a rising star by corporate headquarters. She was honored and excited to be appointed as an internal consultant to work on solving complex systems problems. She knew that this new assignment would be one where she could use her skills to make a difference—and keep learning at the same time.

Terri was assigned to jointly manage a complex audit of the nearby parts manufacturing plant with another consultant, named Nellis. It soon became apparent that Terri and Nellis approached their assignment quite differently. This contributed to early miscommunications with each other and with their client at the plant. Terri raised her concerns directly to Nellis. Initially, he listened carefully and acknowledged her point of view. They made agreements about what each would do differently. Terri worked hard to keep her end of the bargain, but Nellis did not. Terri initiated a second meeting with Nellis to resolve their problems. Again, he appeared to understand her concerns. Again, nothing happened.

Feeling frustrated and worried that the audit would end up behind schedule and poorly organized, she made an appointment to see her boss, Richard. She hoped that he would intervene somehow to get her working relationship with Nellis back on track. During the meeting, Richard seemed distracted and unresponsive to her concerns. After thirty minutes, Richard summed up his point of view. Using an abrupt, irritated tone of voice, he said, "Terri, you are overreacting here. If there is some kind of personality thing between the two of you, that's not my problem. Work it out with Nellis."

"That's what I tried to do," Terri stammered, "but it didn't work." "Well, try again," Richard countered, "and then come back and tell me that this problem is fixed." "Okay, Richard, I will try again," she found herself saying. "I want you to know, I am really going to try to make this work."

Despite the positive sound of this commitment, Terri left Richard's office feeling let down and put down. She went home depressed. The next day at lunch with a co-worker, she couldn't help but express her feelings. When she did, she discovered that, although Richard was considered an effective leader in many regards, he did have a reputation for having trouble with conflict. Either he avoided it altogether or he tried to bulldoze over the issues. Terri's experience was true to the pattern.

After a week of more fruitless conversations with Nellis, Terri felt caught between a rock and a hard place. She scheduled a follow-up meeting with Richard. This time, however, she brought along Pauline, a long-time manager from the plant in whom Richard had a lot of confidence. At their meeting, Pauline told Richard how much effort she had seen Terri put into the audit—and into her relationship with Nellis. She supported Terri's position and made observations about the audit that encouraged immediate action. This time Richard seemed much more attentive to the concerns that were being voiced about the audit. He promised to talk with Nellis right away. Terri left the meeting feeling hopeful. Richard had said that he would do something to get the audit back on track. That was last week—before the memo announcing her reassignment hit her desk.

The day after the memo arrived, Terri was confused and angry. She worried about her credibility and what others must think about her. All the way to work, she fumed through imaginary confrontations with Richard and fantasized about taking her complaints to his boss. When she arrived, she called Richard and left a message that she needed to see him the next morning. She wanted to give herself time to compose her thoughts and prepare for their meeting. She sought help by calling a close friend to act as a sounding board.

As she prepared with her friend, Terri wrestled with her fears and hesi-
tations: What if the conversation took an unexpected turn? What if Richard felt
threatened and started shouting? What if he belittled her as nothing but a
troublemaker? Would her working relationship with him be ruined forever?
Would she have to quit her job? Would speaking up really do any good if
Richard was unwilling to change?

When her friend encouraged her to continue to be open and assertive
with Richard, Terri's nerves flashed warning signs. She said, "But I don't know
where this conversation with Richard might end up. Anything could happen!"
And later, from a more cynical perspective, she said, "You know, this probably
won't do any good. I've tried talking to him already and things have only gotten
worse." She wondered if it was too late to back out of her conversation with
Richard. "I may be wrong about this whole thing. After all, I am new and have
less experience than Nellis. Maybe I should just back off." In the end, her
strong desire to clear up her confusion about her relationship with Richard and
her future in his department swayed her to go ahead.

The next morning, Terri steadied herself and walked into Richard's
office. "Hi, Richard," she said, "I appreciate your making time to see me this
morning." "No problem," he replied. "Come in, Terri, and sit down."

"He seems pretty open," thought Terri. "I guess I'd better get on with
it." With as calm a voice as she could find, Terri proceeded. "Richard, I'm here
because I'm worried about our communication and our working relationship.
These things are very important to me." Richard nodded in agreement. She
continued, "I've been very confused by your recent behavior toward me. We've
had very little direct communication. This all leaves me feeling uncertain about
myself and my place in this organization. It's going to be hard for me to have
the confidence to move into another project until I hear from you about what's
been going on."

After pausing, she added, "A big reason why I am here is that I want to
be treated fairly. Please tell me why you've taken me off the audit, without even
talking to me ahead of time. I need to know if you have a problem with me and
my ability or with how I came to you with my concerns about Nellis. Or is it
something else?" She waited for Richard to speak. When he didn't, she went
on. "In addition to how this makes me feel personally, I'm truly concerned
about the audit." She ended her message by saying, "I would like you to talk to
me about all this."

Her direct, heartfelt statement struck its mark. "Okay," replied Richard.
"You're right. We do need to talk." The conversation that followed was a long
one, in which Richard acknowledged that he also had been deeply frustrated

with the audit. "It's been obvious for a while that you and Nellis don't get along. Nellis has complained to me, too. I've heard things from others at the plant who have noticed the difficulty. It's too bad that this has happened. It got to the point where it was clear that one of you had to move on. Because of the credibility Nellis has in the plant, I decided to move you to another project." Terri was listening carefully, so he went on. "I appreciate your concern that these changes will hurt the audit. But Enrique has worked there many times and is a quick study. I am confident that he and Nellis will do a fine job."

Terri pushed back. "So where does all this leave me, in terms of my job and my credibility with you? With this new assignment, will the scope of my job be changing?" Richard immediately reaffirmed the supportive statements he had made to Terri when he hired her. He said that he had noticed her commitment to the organization and her talent for the work. He described her new project and why he thought she was the best person for the job.

Finally, he admitted that he had not handled the situation as well as he would have liked. "I hate it when these things happen," he confided. "I sometimes have a hard time with conflicts between people. I tend to stay out of them as long as I can. I expect people to take care of their issues on their own. When they don't or can't, it causes me to react." In a more reflective tone, he continued, "I should have called you about my decision, Terri. This part of the issue is really more mine than yours."

As they talked further, they shared their different perspectives about what had happened with the audit. Richard took notes about Terri's views on what should happen next. They also talked about their relationship and how their communication had become distorted. When they finished their conversation, Terri began to feel a shift in their relationship. She sensed that they would be able to communicate more openly in the future. If there were problems, she believed that she would be in a much better position to address them quickly and with less worry.

As she left work that afternoon, she mentally reviewed the situation: "Is this what I wanted? No. Enrique is still going to work with Nellis on the audit and I'll have a new assignment. Is this acceptable? Yes. Because he told me how he viewed me and my performance. He also shared some things with me about why he is the way he is. Does this represent progress? I think so. It sure could have been a lot worse."

Although Terri still felt some doubt, in the long run she saw this as a turning point in her relationship with Richard. Her willingness to speak up increased her respect for both herself and her boss. She was proud of herself for finding the courage to speak up.

Finding Your Courage

To help you in finding the courage to speak up and to develop your skills as a courageous messenger, each of the next five chapters will examine one step of the process. We'll return to Terri's story to illustrate key points. To get the most from this part of the book, we recommend two things:

1. Do not allow too much time between finishing one chapter and starting another; each chapter builds upon the ideas presented in the preceding one.

2. Pick a current (or recent) situation in which you have a message that you would like to bring forward but are hesitant to do so.

Using a personal scenario as a reference point for the material in Chapters Six through Twenty will help you to feel more connected to the steps we describe and to get the most benefit out of reading this book. These chapters and the "Personal Exercises" section of the Messenger's Tool Box contain specific steps to assist you with this important activity. *Please do not neglect to create your own personal case study.*

 PERSONAL EXERCISES

General Exercise 5.1. Reflections on Courage

Story Exercise 5.2. Terri's Challenge

Situation Exercise 5.3. Your Speaking-Up Case Study

KNOW
YOUR TRUE
MESSAGE

CLARIFYING YOUR TRUE
message is an act of
discovery. It requires
looking inside yourself and going beyond the obvious. A message may shift
as a person thinks through what he or
she *really* wants or needs to say. Using
Terri's story as a case in point, this chapter will assist you in finding the three
basic components of your true message.

The Importance of Knowing Your True Message

Knowing your true message is the first step on the pathway of finding the courage to speak up. If you don't know what you want to say, it will be impossible for you to understand your reasons for bringing your message forward or the risks involved. These two points must be clearly understood in order for you to decide whether or not to speak up. If you decide to speak up, clarity about the message will make success more likely. It will help you to see whether your message belongs only to you or represents the concerns of many people. You may find that what you at first thought was a single point of concern actually touches on larger issues or systems problems. Such insights can make a difference in terms of how you bring your message forward.

Basic Components of a True Message

A true message shares information and requests or suggests action to be taken by the receiver. An effective formula for the message includes a description of:

1. A situation, specifically a problem, concern, or opportunity

2. The impact of the situation

3. A request or suggestion for action

In its best form, it is:

- Honest

- Clear

- Direct

- Tactful

- Nondefensive

- Focused on the core of the messenger's concerns or ideas

We use the phrase *true* message because the circumstances that inspire a messenger to speak up can generate many points that could be said. A true message conveys the most important points. It is what the messenger truly wants the receiver to hear, understand, remember, and act upon.

How to Discover Your True Message

To discover the three component parts of your message—the situation you are concerned about, its impacts, and your recommendation for action—we suggest doing five things, in consecutive order:

1. Assess your situation and its impacts.

2. Explore possible underlying causes for the situation.

3. List possible actions that your receiver could take that would help to move things forward in a positive way.

4. Draft your message, using language you might use if you decide to present your message.

5. Determine the importance of delivering your message.

Figure 6.1 shows another way to represent this sequence.

Step One: Assess Your Situation and Its Impacts

When you are thinking about the situation that inspires you to speak up and the impacts that situation is having on you and

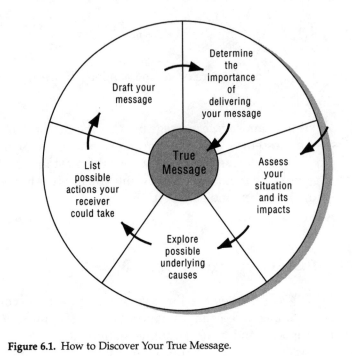

Figure 6.1. How to Discover Your True Message.

others, it is helpful to return to the model presented in Chapter Three. Figure 3.1 highlighted three areas that typically make up the content of tough messages. A set of phrases was offered to help define *work outcomes, working relationships, and personal behavior.* A quick review of this list can jog your thinking and help you to focus in on the essential elements of your situation and its impacts. As you read through the list, ask yourself:

- What is going on that makes me want to speak up?
- What impacts have resulted from this situation?
- What aspects of the situation and its impacts are most important to me?

As you think about the message you want to bring forward, it is helpful to remember the following things:

- The initial situation that inspires your message can be in any area.

- The impact of the problem, concern, or opportunity you have identified can be in any area.

- Your description of the impact is what will capture your receiver's attention and inspire interest and cooperation.

- A message will be more powerful if it describes an impact in an area that is important to the receiver; this can vary depending on the receiver's responsibilities, values, and personality.

- Generally speaking, when presenting a tough message to someone with a greater level of responsibility, the most powerful impact statement will include work outcomes.

- The more areas of impact, the more complex your message may become; you may have to work harder to get to the core of what you want to say to your receiver.

There is no right or wrong way to proceed with your assessment. Some people like to take notes, some prefer to talk things out, and some can keep track of things in their head. Imagine being in Terri's place as she thinks through the situation and its possible impacts. She writes out her thoughts and then organizes them around a few key themes. After reviewing her completed list, she uses check marks to indicate the aspects that are most important to her.

The situation I'm concerned about

Richard decided to replace me on the audit with Enrique without talking to me about it. ✓

Richard's initial response to my request for help with Nellis was nonsupportive and caused me to feel put down.

The impact the situation is having on me and others

On my work:
I am having difficulty concentrating on my work because of all this confusion. ✓

On the audit:
Bringing Enrique in at this late date will slow down the audit.

People in the plant will get confused about the audit process and results. ✓

On my relationship with Richard:
Has our relationship been damaged by all this? Will we be able to work well together in the future? There's a possible loss of trust and respect on both sides. ✓

On me:
I'm confused about my value to the organization. ✓

I worry that my career will be hurt by all this; I have lots of stress.

I feel lousy about myself and my ability to communicate.

Terri's initial analysis of the situation indicates that the focus of her concern is Richard's personal behavior, including how he performs his job of being her supervisor and his lack of communication with her. Yet the impacts of his behavior are seen in two other areas, *work outcomes,* related to her work and the audit's success, and *working relationships,* pertaining to her relationship with Richard, her future in the organization, and her feelings about herself.

Getting clear on these aspects, Terri can see that her message is a complex one in which all three possible message content areas overlap. This is a clue to Terri that she will need to carefully sort out her true message so that if she meets with Richard she can be clear with him about her concerns. This is particularly so because many emotions are involved on her part.

Step Two: Explore Possible Underlying Causes for the Situation

The three components of the message formula do not include a statement about what might have caused the situation. However, exploring such possibilities is necessary background work that will contribute directly to your recommendation for action and will prepare you to offer your perspective or respond to your receiver's questions about the causes of the problem if your conversation focuses on solving it.

A question to ask yourself is: "What might have caused or contributed to the situation that I want to help improve?" It is important to note that most answers to this question will be guesses or assumptions, rather than acknowledged facts. By yourself or working with someone as a sounding board: (1) list as many possible reasons as you can, (2) sort them into categories that capture the themes in your list, and (3) review the list to identify the most *probable* causes.

Returning to Terri's situation, we can see a wide range of possible causes for Richard's behavior. In this case, her responses could be divided into groupings about events that might have happened, possible aspects of Richard's character and skills, and views that Richard might hold about Terri. The check marks indicate the causes that seem most probable, given what she knows, believes, and has experienced.

What might have happened

Nellis has complained to Richard about me and that has influenced him.

Richard doesn't want to get involved in an interpersonal conflict and has taken the easy way out by assigning Enrique to work with Nellis. ✓

Richard might be mad about my speaking up and has reassigned me as a result. ✓

Nellis and Richard know something about the work that will make it difficult for me to continue and be successful and that Richard is uncomfortable telling me about.

53

Richard's character or skills

Richard doesn't like dealing directly with someone when he has concerns about that person's performance.

Richard is not sensitive to how he comes across to others. ✓

Richard's views about me

Richard doesn't see me as competent. ✓

Richard doesn't want to help me to succeed.

Richard is carrying a grudge against me for complaining about Nellis.

Richard thinks I can handle things on my own and don't need his active attention. ✓

Terri identifies many possible reasons that *might* be behind Richard's behavior. In doing so, her assumptions about Richard and his intentions range from positive to neutral to negative. Because Terri does not solely focus on her negative feelings about Richard, she enables herself to do a more objective analysis of what might actually underlie Richard's behavior. This will be an asset to her as she attempts to construct a message that is honest, tactful, and nondefensive.

Please note that a caution is in order on this point. If you find that most of your probable reasons for the situation make strong negative assumptions about your receiver's or others' intentions, you are in the middle of a tough case. An example of this would be if Terri strongly believed that Richard was intentionally manipulating her. If you find yourself in this situation, you may want to delay your decision to speak up until you read Part Three, "Acting with Courage," and Part Four, "The Tough Cases." Then return to Chapter Ten for assistance with making a decision.

Step Three: List Possible Actions That Your Receiver Could Take

The focus for this list should be actions that would move things forward in a positive direction. These recommendations are typically tied to (1) the effects of the situation and (2) the probable reasons behind the problem, concern, or opportunity.

Prior to building your list of suggestions, ask yourself, "Given the items I have identified as most significant and most probable, what action do I want my receiver to take?" This question focuses your list of actions so that your request addresses underlying causes or helps to reduce the negative impacts. For example, given the items Terri checked, her list might include the following:

What Richard could do to help things move forward

He could tell me his reasons for replacing me with Enrique without talking to me.

He could listen to my side of the story.

He could give me feedback on how he sees my abilities and contributions.

He could tell me whether or not all this has damaged our relationship or my chances to be successful.

In identifying the actions she might ask Richard to take, Terri did not become bogged down by the two causes that reflected negative assumptions about Richard. This is an important step on Terri's part. If you find that your recommended actions are based on strong negative assumptions, it will be hard for you to suggest these steps without threatening your receiver. This threat will occur if your negative assumptions leak through into the conversation. Should this happen, it could easily be construed by your receiver as an indirect attack, shutting down the conversation and any hope for change. Again, if this describes your situation, you are facing a tough case.

Step Four: Draft Your Message

Next, it is time to develop a draft of the message you want your receiver to hear, understand, remember, and act upon. As you decide what points you want to make, it is important to work with the language you may use if you decide to present your message. Three questions will help you to sort through the overlapping issues you, like Terri, may have identified in your assessment. Your purpose is to decide what is most important for you to convey to your receiver.

1. What is honest and at the core of my ideas or concerns?

2. What is honest and can be expressed in a tactful, nondefensive way?

3. What will be most likely to gain my receiver's interest and cooperation?

To answer these questions, first, think about the three components of a message: the situation, its impacts, and your request or suggestion for action; second, review all your thoughts or the notes you have taken, screening out the side issues and looking only for the *vital few elements* that are most important for your receiver to hear; and third, once they have been identified, succinctly write them together using words you might say to your receiver. For example, in Terri's case it would be:

The situation

Richard's behavior toward me has me worried. He seemed very unresponsive when I approached him about my concerns. I left feeling put down. Then he pulled me off the audit without talking to me in advance.

Its effects

This has caused me to feel uncertain about myself and my work. I can't seem to concentrate on anything while I have all these worries and confusion, and it is very hard to think about a new assignment.

I've begun to question my ability to do quality work or to communicate effectively.

I am worried that my relationship with Richard will be negative and mistrustful from now on.

I worry that all this may be a sign that my career in this organization is significantly limited—or over.

Request or suggestion for action

I would like Richard to tell me why he pulled me off the audit without talking to me ahead of time. If he has lost confidence in me because of the concerns I brought about Nellis and the audit, then I need to know what options I have in terms of my work in this department or in the company.

Notice how Terri's language is descriptive in a neutral way. She does not choose words that blame or suggest suspicion about Richard's intentions. Yet she does not soften the core of her message—Richard's behavior and the negative impact it has had on her.

Step Five: Determine the Importance of Delivering Your Message

Just because a message has been clarified does not mean that it is important to deliver it. Key factors influencing its importance will be illuminated by answering these two questions: "Given everything else going on in my work life, how important is it to deliver my message?" and "Why do I give it this level of importance?" Before answering, return to the draft of your message. The impacts that you have seen will guide your decision about the importance of delivering the message. Backing up to the lists that you developed about underlying causes may also provide some insight. The following criteria may be useful:

- *Very important:* If these issues are not addressed, it will be hard for me to attend to other things.

57

- *Moderately important:* This is not the most important work-related concern I currently have, but it does deserve my time, attention, and energy.

- *Not very important:* Many other more important things deserve my time, attention, and energy.

For Terri, delivering her message was close to being the most important work she could do. She was unable to concentrate on her work and was beginning to doubt herself, her relationship with her boss, and her career in the organization.

Terri gave herself a day to mull over the issues reflected in her notes. She wanted to bring forth her concerns honestly and assertively, without unnecessarily offending Richard. By carefully assessing the situation, its impacts, and what action she wanted from Richard, she was able to focus on the most important aspects. She could start her conversation with a sincere and straightforward statement and a request that was successful in engaging Richard's interest and cooperation.

PERSONAL EXERCISES

Situation Exercise 6.1. Your True Message

Situation Exercise 6.2. Did the Process Work for You?

Situation Exercise 6.3. Testing for a Direct, Tactful Message

KNOW
YOUR REAL
MOTIVATION

PEOPLE DELIVER TOUGH messages all the time. Even to unreceptive receivers. Even in the face of unpleasant and likely repercussions. They shake themselves out of their comfort zone to speak up because of important, heartfelt motivations. These powerful reasons are strong enough to overcome worries about potential negative consequences.

Without the spark of such motivation, many problems that concern people at work would show little improvement.

What Is Your Real Motivation?

Your real motivation is the *core reason*—or reasons—why you want to speak up about your message. Another way to think of this is to look at the benefits that will come to you and others if your receiver addresses your concerns by taking the action you have suggested. Discovering your real motivation is similar to clarifying your true message: after thoughtful consideration, you may realize motives that you had not originally understood. Depending on the complexity of the issues, it can take some focused time and effort to discover the reason that *most* compels you to deliver your message. Getting to that core is what this chapter is all about.

Although motivations vary from person to person, *they are usually positive,* centering on some type of improvement or learning that will lead to positive change. However, some messengers do bring forward their messages in order to hurt or manipulate others. A few observations and cautions about this type of motivation will be found at the end of the chapter.

Why Is It Important to Understand Your Real Motivation?

It can be very easy for messengers to be labeled as troublemakers. After all, they often put uncomfortable subjects on the table for discussion. Their messages suggest that change is needed. They frequently speak passionately about their ideas or experiences. Each of these actions can be irritating—if not threatening—to those who are happy with the status quo. The difference between being viewed as a helpful colleague or a troublemaker may come down to this single question: "What does your receiver believe about your reasons for raising a sensitive subject?"

Receivers are less inclined to listen or respond positively to messengers who bring tough news with motives that are perceived as: unclear or confused, undisclosed or secretive, or based solely on self-interest.

These are the situations in which messengers often "get shot." These "shootings" often are done by a receiver who, for whatever reason, doubts the messenger's intentions. When a messenger confidently and sincerely communicates her or his motives along with the message, the confusion or suspicion that may exist in the receiver's mind is likely to be reduced, if not eliminated altogether. If you want to be successful as a messenger, look inside yourself in order to understand the fundamental reasons for your decision to speak up. If you decide to go ahead, this clarity will enable you to confidently express your motivation in ways that will be credible to your receiver.

What Are the Benefits to Yourself and Others of Being a Messenger?

People speak up because they see a benefit in doing so. Benefits can come to: the messenger, the receiver, others connected to the issue, and the organization.

Messengers *always* have some type of self-interest that is served by speaking up. When they are asked about their reasons for speaking up, people will commonly describe a desire to:

- Address issues of fairness or equity

- Save time or money

- Make things easier or more efficient

- Create a more pleasant work environment

- Serve customers better

- Provide better quality

61

- Help others
- Live up to the expectations of their job or their supervisor
- Create an opportunity to learn or have new experiences
- Build relationships

Sometimes messengers operate from a benefit that is intangible and hard to see, except by those who know the messenger well. But underneath, the messenger's self-esteem and integrity are enhanced because of "doing what's right."

How to Discover Your Real Motivation

These four useful steps will help you to discover the powerful core of your motivation to speak up:

1. Identify the benefits to yourself and others.
2. Clarify your reasons for speaking up.
3. Pinpoint your real motivation.
4. Determine the strength of your real motivation.

These separate but compatible steps build on each other, as Figure 7.1 suggests.

Step One: Identify the Benefits to Yourself and Others

A messenger who senses a need or an opportunity to speak up typically has a general idea of the good things that might result. An analytic approach can yield fairly detailed insights about the possible positive results. To illustrate, imagine being in Terri's

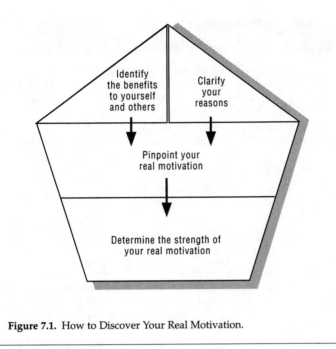

Figure 7.1. How to Discover Your Real Motivation.

shoes as she thinks about the benefits that would come if she delivers her message to Richard. The results might look like those in Grid 7.1.

After filling in the grid, Terri reviews it and indicates with check marks the items that are the most important to her. Identifying benefits such as these is a highly subjective process that has no right or wrong answers. Yet the more willing you are to look inside yourself and push beyond your first response, the more clarity you can gain about what is important to you.

Step Two: Clarify Your Reasons for Speaking Up—
The Five Why's

Another approach to understanding your real motivation is to ask five times in succession: "Why do I want to bring this message forward?" To do this revealing exercise:

Who Benefits	What Are the Benefits?
The Messenger	Clarity about where I stand with Richard will help me to know what is going on. If I can succeed in this department, it will help me to make decisions about what I should do next and ease some of my anxiety about the unknown. ✓ Richard may change his behavior and become more communicative with me; with more information and support, I could do a better job. Being treated fairly is important to me; I will feel better about myself if I do my part to ensure that this happens. ✓
The Receiver	Richard will gain information about how his behavior has a negative impact on some people, me included; this may trigger some growth and change on his part. ✓ He will benefit from improved performance on my part. Perhaps Richard will gain more insight into the audit and its current problems.
Others in the Organization	When I'm at my best, I have lots of energy and ideas that can help others.
The Organization	I have a contribution to make to the organization and I want to help this place be successful. ✓ If we have better communication and cooperation in our department, the rest of the organization will benefit from our improved teamwork. If I can convince Richard that I should continue with the audit, it will go more smoothly and quickly than if Enrique steps in and it starts over.

Grid 7.1. What Are the Benefits of Speaking Up?

1. State an initial reason for bringing your message forward.

2. Then say why that reason is important.

3. Then, again, say why *that* reason is important.

4. Repeat this process until you get to the fifth level of reasoning.

You may find that you start repeating yourself. If this happens, you will know that you have found a core reason for speaking up. This is a good exercise to talk through with a friend who can play the role of an interviewer, asking you "And why is that reason important?" If Terri had done this exercise, she might have recorded her thoughts in the following way:

Why am I willing to bring this message forward?

First why: *Because I need to know why Richard took me off the audit without even talking to me about it.*

And why is that important?
Second why: *Because this action seems to fit with some of our other communication. I'm beginning to see a pattern that doesn't make me feel very good about the future of our working relationship.*

And why is that important?
Third why: *This uncertainty makes it hard for me to concentrate on my work and makes me feel like a failure.* ✓

And why is that important?
Fourth why: *Because I don't know if I've done something wrong or not. If I have, I need to know it. If I haven't, then I'm being treated unfairly.*

And why is that important?
Fifth why: *Because I deserve to be treated fairly. Everybody does.* ✓

The "five why's" can elicit clarity about one's motivation and values. After looking at the flow of her messages, Terri checked the reasons that have the most meaning to her.

65

Step Three: Pinpoint Your Real Motivation

If you review Terri's benefits grid and her "five-why's" list, you will see some common points. Because these two exercises approach the topic of motivation from different perspectives, they provide an interesting counterpoint to one another. Comparing the results is a great way to find the answer to the question: "Of all the good reasons for speaking up, what most compels you to do so?"

In Terri's case, of her six check marks, four reasons appear as most important, two of which were on both lists. At the core of her motivation, she wants and needs:

- Clarity about her relationship and communication with Richard
- To be treated fairly

These are her real motivations. She clearly addressed both in her conversation with Richard. Other important issues are her hope that Richard may gain insights that will trigger some personal growth and behavioral changes and her strong desire to make a contribution to the organization's success.

As you examine your motivation for speaking up, you may not find such a neat overlap between the two approaches. In that case, look for any themes or patterns of connection among the benefits and reasons that you have checked as most significant. These patterns will point you to your real motivation for speaking up.

Step Four: Determine the Strength of Your Real Motivation

When you decide whether or not to speak up, the strength of your motivation will be compared to the repercussions and other reasons that cause you to hesitate. Whichever is stronger will determine, in large part, if you will go ahead. A question you might ask yourself is "What amount of discomfort or disruption am I willing to experience in order to follow through on my motivation to speak up?" For example:

- "A lot of discomfort or disruption" indicates that your motivation is *very important* to you and that it is worth facing uncomfortable situations that might lead to immediate or delayed repercussions.

- "A small amount of discomfort or disruption" suggests that your motivation is *moderately important*, but that you are not willing to undergo much sacrifice to realize the benefits of delivering your message.

- "No discomfort or disruption" points to a *low level of motivation* that would not stand up to the risks that are likely to occur.

Terri's main reasons—her relationship with her boss, her future in the organization, her sense of fairness, and her self-esteem—go straight to the center of her work experience. These are powerful motivational factors that are worth risking some level of discomfort and disruption for. Terri would most likely classify her real motivation as "very important."

Motivations That Are Overly Self-Focused or Intentionally Hurtful to Others

Cautions are in order in two situations. If, after reflecting on your motivation for speaking up, you realize (1) that your real reasons are overly self-focused and that the true benefits will only come to you at the expense of others or (2) that your motivation is to hurt or manipulate others, then slow down and think twice about bringing your message forward. If you proceed, your chances of being successful are limited. And if you are intentionally trying to hurt someone through speaking up, you are likely to seriously damage your relationships.

As you reflect further, keep in mind that personal interests and benefits are not wrong. There is no reason why you should not speak up to ask for something that you want or need. Just because you can't find a payoff for the organization or someone else is no reason to remain silent. The problem arises when self-focused interests come across as selfish, power-oriented, or destructive. Asking to change an unpopular rule or requesting a pay raise are not bad things. But it is a different story altogether when such a message is seen as a means of manipulating or diminishing some person or effort.

Messengers may find that their motives are mixed. Their reasons include, for example, both getting even with someone and accomplishing a change that benefits others or the organization. If you find yourself in this situation, honestly admit this combination of motivations. Then try to set the hurtful reason aside. Recognize its potential to undermine your conversation. You will need to be very honest about why you are coming forward so that your receiver can trust the positive side of your intentions.

 PERSONAL EXERCISES

Situation Exercise 7.1. Your Real Motivation

Situation Exercise 7.2. Did the Process Work for You?

General Exercise 7.3. Hurtful Messages

ASSESS
YOUR RISK

O
NCE YOU ARE CLEAR
on your message
and motives, you
can gain courage through a careful
analysis of the risks you face. Ultimately,
these risks must be compared with your
motivation for speaking up. If you
decide that your goal is worth it, you will
go forward. But unless the nature of the
risks is determined, you will not be able
to make a confident comparison between
the two choices. This chapter offers a
rational process to apply to this slippery,
highly emotional subject.

The Risk of Repercussions

Fears point to the risks messengers anticipate. These risks are reflected in what messengers think about when they are trying to decide whether or not to speak up. When messengers say out loud the worries that go on in their head, it can sound like this: "If I say what I *really* think, . . .

"Will something bad happen to me, now or later?"

"Will I look like a fool?"

"Will people get mad at me?"

"Will the situation turn into an argument that only makes things worse?"

"Will anything really change, or will this just be a wasted effort?"

"Will others who depend on me get hurt?"

To get more specific, if you ask someone, "What are you *afraid of losing* by saying what is really on your mind?" the answers often fall into one of three categories:

1. Damaged or lost credibility or reputation

2. Damaged or lost relationships

3. Decreased security (job security, financial security, or physical security)

These are the *repercussions*, the *negative consequences*, that people often fear will happen. As children, we learn that negative consequences are associated with saying things naturally. Most of us learn these early lessons well, so as adults working in organizations, we hesitate—sometimes unnecessarily—to say things that need to be said. For the purposes of this book, *risk* is defined as the likelihood that repercussions or other negative consequences will, in fact, happen as the result of speaking up.

As you move ahead to define the risks you face as a messenger, four points are worth remembering:

1. Risk cannot be eliminated but it can be *understood.*

2. Once risk has been understood, it can be balanced with the motivation to go ahead.

3. Risk cannot be fully predicted, but careful thought allows a realistic estimate of the present risk.

4. Moving ahead involves acceptance of risk—being okay with the repercussions that might occur.

Some Situations Carry More Risk Than Others

Predicting the risk associated with speaking up is the tough part. Predictions, after all, are only predictions. However, a set of factors exists that, if present, might suggest a greater *probability* that some type of repercussion will result. As you review this list, think about the personal speaking-up case study you identified at the end of Chapter Five and in Situation Exercise 5.3. Which of these factors might be present?

- Is your receiver someone who does not like to receive negative feedback or hear about problems?

- Is your message one that your receiver is likely to find very disturbing?

- Is your receiver your supervisor or someone who has direct influence over your job?

- Is mistrust a noticeable element of your relationship with your receiver?

- Does your receiver have a tendency to hold grudges or take reprisals?

- Do you have a reputation as a troublemaker or a whiner?

- Are you different in some way from most of the others in your organization (as in your gender, race, sexual orientation, life-style, politics, age, or personal or professional background)? Do these characteristics make communication more difficult?

- Have you been associated in the past with controversial issues that have a lingering negative impact?

- In other tense situations, have you found yourself losing control of your emotions?

- Does your organization avoid problems?

- Is your organization one that tends to assign blame?

Remember that just because any of these factors might be present, a repercussion is not a foregone conclusion. Think about driving on a cold, rainy night. Just because the roads are slick and the lighting is poor does not mean that an accident will occur. Yet intelligent drivers know enough to be more cautious and more conscious in these hazardous situations. The same holds true for skillful messengers. When they recognize environmental hazards that might make a repercussion more likely, they proceed with greater caution and consciousness.

Returning to Terri's circumstances, we might well assume that she sees these risk factors:

Richard probably won't like to hear that I'm complaining about how he handled this decision. He may think I'm questioning his decision.

Richard is my boss; he could have a lot of power over my career.

Because I am relatively new and unproven in this department, it would be easy for him or others to label me as a troublemaker or incompetent.

As Terri moves ahead to more specifically define her risks, she may use these factors to stimulate her thinking about the possible downside of speaking up.

How to Assess Your Risk

The process for assessing your risk involves the following five steps:

1. Identify the repercussions you believe might happen.
2. Define your evidence for anticipating these repercussions.
3. Evaluate how recent the evidence is.
4. Determine the similarities between your past and present speaking-up situations.
5. Determine whether your worries about repercussions are realistic.

Figure 8.1 shows another way to see the relationships between these suggestions.

Step One: Identify the Repercussions You Believe Might Happen

The first step in your risk assessment is to identify the repercussions you believe are most likely to occur if something negative happens. Be as objective as you can. Don't just create a laundry list of all the negative things that are *possible*. You might ask yourself: "Given what I know about my situation and work environment, what repercussions are *probable?*"

When Terri carefully considered the probable repercussions associated with delivering her message, she found five:

Figure 8.1. How to Assess Your Risk.

I might be ignored or put down again, just like the first time I talked to Richard about my problems with Nellis.

Richard might get angry with me for bringing this up.

I might be labeled a troublemaker for complaining about how I was taken off the audit.

My job scope could be reduced, with fewer opportunities to progress.

I might lose credibility with a lot of people, hurting my career.

Once the repercussions have been named, you are ready to examine them more fully to see how valid your worries about them might be. Try not to clump or group the repercussions, as this can hide important elements of your analysis. Take your time and be thorough. The question that you must ask for each repercussion is "How realistic is my fear that this will happen?" The next three steps are designed to answer this question.

Step Two: Define Your Evidence for Anticipating These Repercussions

When you list probable repercussions, you have certain *evidence* for predicting that they might happen. This type of evidence is the set of *reasons* why you think a repercussion is probable. By evaluating your reasons, you will have a more informed sense of whether your worries about certain repercussions are realistic.

The first test is to compare each probable repercussion with your past experiences. Consider the following scale and where you might place your evidence that these repercussions could occur:

Higher risk   *Lower risk*

$$\longleftarrow \joinrel\longrightarrow$$

Compelling personal   **Circumstantial**   **Worst-case thinking**
experience   **or indirect evidence**

Compelling personal experience means that the repercussion you are considering:

- Has happened to you before or you have personally observed it happening to someone else

- Came from the same receiver

For example, Terri knows that when she came to Richard with her concerns about working with Nellis, he told her that she was overreacting and dismissed her concerns as a "personality problem." The two events—speaking up about difficulties with Nellis and being put down—are fully linked in Terri's mind. Terri could clearly recall the edge of anger in Richard's voice. Compelling personal experience is like that—direct, immediate, and memorable—even if the repercussion occurred some time after the fact. Terri sees no other possible explanation. One event caused the other to occur.

Circumstantial or indirect evidence represents a belief, but not a certainty, that repercussions have occurred in the past. This may have happened in several ways:

- You personally experienced or observed something happen but other explanations were possible besides repercussions.

- Someone shared a personal experience of repercussions that you did not observe.

- Someone described personal repercussions that were *believed* to have happened.

- Someone described repercussions that someone else experienced, observed, or heard about.

For example, after Terri brought Pauline with her to meet with Richard, Terri was replaced on the audit. Regardless of how that looks, she knows that Richard could have made this decision for other reasons. Yet it is *possible, though not certain,* that Richard took her off the audit because she brought forward her concerns. If this is what occurred, continuing to speak up may inspire Richard to further reduce the scope of her job.

Circumstantial evidence requires a judgment call about what has happened and how much weight you, as a messenger, will give others' experience. There is no absolute cause-and-effect link between speaking up and a negative consequence. But the environment might suggest that a connection *could* exist. Keep in mind that circumstantial evidence covers a broad range, extending from near-compelling personal experience to something close to worst-case thinking.

Worst-case thinking does not depend much on past experiences or the influence of others. It often starts from a small piece of information (sometimes gossip), an event, or someone's behavior. From that information, event, or behavior, a great deal more is *inferred*—in a negative direction. When someone jumps to a negative conclusion, she or he demonstrates worst-case thinking. Some messengers may have very little real evidence upon which to base the prediction that a particular repercussion might happen. The prediction is based primarily on imaginable possibilities that are connected very loosely to something that may or may not have actually happened. This category of evidence is very common in stressful and ambiguous circumstances, which provide few clues about what is going on or what could happen.

Terri reflected worst-case thinking when she worried about being labeled a troublemaker, losing her credibility, and damaging her career for good. She had no evidence that anyone's career in her company had ever been damaged in this way because that person challenged a manager. When people worry about such things happening in the absence of compelling or circumstantial evidence, they are not being realistic. Worst-case fears undermine an effective evaluation of the actual risks.

Notice, however, how natural it would be for Terri to slide into worst-case thinking because she did not yet have an explanation about why she was taken off the audit. Worst-case thinking multiplies the worries associated with compelling personal experience and circumstantial evidence. Some circumstantial evidence plus some worst-case thinking creates a dangerous combination. Add a dash of compelling personal experience, even if it is not directly related, and the worst-case repercussions can feel inevitable.

Step Three: Evaluate How Recent the Evidence Is

The next test of your evidence is to ask yourself: "How recently has an example of this repercussion taken place?" This question asks you to consider how much things may have changed over time. These changes may pertain to you, your receiver, or the dynamics and priorities of your organization. The question is based on the assumption that the further back you have to go in time to find a similar repercussion, the less likely it is that the repercussion will happen again. Again, a sliding scale encourages you to examine whether your predictions are based on the very recent past (within six months) or on history (several years ago).

Higher risk   *Lower risk*

<——>

Very recent   **Some time ago**   **History**

Thinking about this scale provides an excellent opportunity to check out how much weight your past experiences have with you. All of us are subject to carrying around a certain amount of "baggage." If you experienced severe or painful repercussions years ago, you may still be burdened with strong feelings of anger, resentment, or hurt. These painful experiences can cause you to be more cautious about taking risks. Through this examination, however, you may discover that you, your receiver, and your situation have changed radically. If so, acknowledging that these changes have lightened your load may help you to proceed with greater courage and enthusiasm.

Terri could see that her experiences with put-downs and anger were quite recent. Once more, they emerged as high-risk elements of her situation. Her concerns about her job being reduced in scope, because she had just been removed from the audit, also were on the higher-risk side of the scale. However, she realized that repercussions related to permanent damage to her career had not occurred in her experience lately—or at all.

Step Four: Determine the Similarities Between Your Past and Present Speaking-Up Situations

A last sliding scale asks you to identify the past situation in which your probable repercussion took place. Once you have done this, you can compare the characteristics of the past incident to those you currently face. Essentially, this asks you: "How are these two situations similar or different?" Key points to consider include:

- Your receiver

- Your workplace

- Your message

- Your motivation

- Your life experiences and skills

- Others who could influence the situation

The more the current scenario repeats a past one in which the repercussions actually happened, the greater the potential risk this time.

Higher risk   *Lower risk*

◄───►

Very similar   **Somewhat similar**   **Not similar at all**

Terri decides that she is on the higher-risk side of the scale for probable put-downs and anger by Richard, and for possible reduction to the scope of her job. If she delivers her message, she will again be coming to Richard with questions and problems that involve his decisions and performance as a leader. She believes that, in effect, she will be repeating her first and second meetings with him. If anything, she will be placing even more pressure on him to explain himself and what he is doing. Her worries about being labeled a troublemaker and about long-term damage, however, don't even fit on the scale. They haven't ever happened to Terri or anyone she knows well at work.

Step Five: Determine Whether Your Worries About Repercussions Are Realistic

With the examination of your probable repercussions complete, you are ready to integrate your conclusions in order to answer the question: "Just how realistic are these fears or worries?" If you have evaluated several repercussions against each of the three scales, you have many possibilities to consider. As you track your responses, it is important to look for the trends. The more your responses fall on the left-hand side of the scales, the higher your risk and the more realistic your worries. If they fall toward the right, the risk is not likely to be as high and the worries are less realistic.

In Terri's case, she evaluated all five probable repercussions, marking the scales as follows:

◄──►

Compelling personal experience	Circumstantial or indirect experience	Worst-case thinking
Put-downs	Job could be reduced in scope	Being labeled a troublemaker
Anger		Hurting my career for good

◄──►

Very recent	Some time ago	History
Put-downs		
Anger		
Job could be reduced in scope		

◄──►

Very similar	Somewhat similar	Not similar at all
Put-downs		
Anger		
Job could be reduced in scope		

As she puts these pieces together, Terri sees the most uncomfortable elements of risk in her situation in the following way: First, if she is going to experience any repercussions, they are most likely to consist of put-downs or some kind of angry response. A second, and more serious, concern is that her job might be reduced in scope. Although her evidence is circumstantial, these are the repercussions that scare Terri the most. However, she has no solid evidence that her long-term career will be affected or that she will be labeled a troublemaker.

Terri must face up to these fears if she is going to proceed with her meeting with Richard. She now has a more defined perspective of the risk, but this is a painful moment. Her analysis tells her that she may face a difficult meeting and that, if it doesn't work out, she may pay a price in her assignments. Courage will be required if she goes ahead.

Balancing Your Risk Against Your Motivation: Look at Contingencies First

At this point, a messenger is ready to consider how the risks stack up against the power of personal motivation. Before addressing that larger issue, however, you may wish to think through your contingency plans by asking yourself: "How will I respond if the likely repercussions come to pass?" If thinking about contingency plans causes you to step back, take the time to do so. If you cannot accept the repercussions you face, there is no point in proceeding—no matter how strong your motivation. If you feel that you do not need contingency plans or if you can think of how you will respond in a constructive way, you are willing to take the risks.

Terri thought very carefully about how she might handle Richard's put-downs if they occurred. She also considered what she would do if, by the end of the meeting, she felt that Richard had responded negatively to her concerns about their communication and working relationship. She could see herself doing two things. If Richard got angry or engaged in put-downs, she would immediately ask him to stop this behavior. If she determined that her efforts to communicate were not received positively, she would make a conscious effort to think through what she had observed and learned about Richard. She would go back to Pauline for advice and she would consider her job options in light of her discoveries.

With these contingency plans in mind, Terri was able to accept the repercussions that might come from her conversation and was ready to weigh her risks and motivations. When you are in this situation, it is time to ask yourself: "Are my reasons for speaking up important enough to outweigh the repercussions that realistically might happen?"

Terri thought about this question and noted:

Until this uncertainty about my relationship with Richard and my job is cleared up, I will not feel good about my work or myself. That's a lot worse than what I may have to face in this meeting. I need to know if I have already lost credibility with Richard and if my new assignment means that the scope of my job has been reduced. If these negative consequences have not happened, I need to know why the change was made so that I can learn from this situation. Getting clear on these things is worth the risk I've identified.

Additionally, Terri felt that speaking up was a way to show respect for herself. If she did not treat herself fairly and with respect, she could not expect others to do the same.

As you know from her story in Chapter Five, Terri's predictions of repercussions did not come true. Her analysis, after all, was based on what might happen *if* something went wrong. She found the courage to speak up, however, by facing what realistically might come her way.

 PERSONAL EXERCISES

Situation Exercise 8.1. Your Risk Factors

Situation Exercise 8.2. Assess Your Risk

General Exercise 8.3. Instances of Worst-Case Thinking

Situation Exercise 8.4. Your Contingency Plans

Situation Exercise 8.5. Did the Process Work for You?

9

UNDERSTAND YOUR YES-BUTS

IN THE LAST CHAPTER, you identified the risks you may actually be taking by speaking up. If you realized that the power of your motivation was greater than the realistic repercussions you might experience, yet you *still* found yourself hesitating to move ahead with your message, it is time to consider the other barriers that may stand in your way. Perhaps you are listening to "yes-buts"—self-imposed doubts that, if voiced, would sound like: "Yes, but if I speak up, ..."

"It won't do any good."

"She won't really change."

"It may mean more work for me."

"I'm not sure I'm right."

"I don't want to cause anybody any trouble."

"It's not my job to do this."

"No one else is willing to speak up about this, so why should I?"

"I wasn't brought up to confront people directly."

"I don't have the skills to be effective."

"I don't know where the conversation will end up."

"I've never done this before."

What Are Yes-Buts and Why Are They Important?

Yes-buts are all the reasons that keep you from speaking up other than your fears about repercussions. A second-level obstacle to acting with courage, yes-buts are first cousins to risks. Rather than reflecting a messenger's fears of negative consequences, they identify cracks in the messenger's confidence or willingness to proceed. They have to do with how we have been conditioned to respond to life's events.

There is nothing wrong with yes-buts. They are a part of the logic that shapes everyday decisions and activities. However, it is important to understand them. If they are left unexamined, you may miss an opportunity to identify:

■ Another fear or risk that is hidden behind a yes-but

■ A superficial reason for not speaking up that can feel more powerful than the motivation for moving ahead and become a convenient excuse

■ A broader issue about patterns of thinking and behaving that you may want to change

The second item mentioned is of great concern to us. Not speaking up, with no actual threats or solid reasons to prevent a person from doing so, represents a great loss. Others lose out on hearing ideas or concerns that might trigger a variety of workplace improvements, and you may have unconsciously stifled yourself by imposing unnecessary limits on your interactions. There is no payoff in either of these situations.

Yes-Buts: An Opportunity for Personal Change

As you go beneath the surface, looking to see if a yes-but reveals an additional risk or an excuse for inaction, you may discover the third option: a well-developed, but sometimes hidden, pattern of thinking or behaving that may act as an internal defense against changing the status quo. If you sense that this may be true for you, focus your exploration by asking yourself: "Do my yes-buts remind me of other situations I've been in and suggest a pattern that may be counterproductive for me?"

As with some of the points raised previously, exploring this more obscure personal terrain can become uncomfortable. Yet ultimately it can shed light on your individual makeup, background, and patterns of thinking and behaving. You may reflect on how you grew up or remember some of the significant teachings passed on by influential family members, teachers, or early supervisors. In such moments, yes-buts represent opportunities for self-knowledge and growth.

Shifting from Control to Influence

Some of the most commonly voiced yes-buts have to do with control. This important issue may unexpectedly surface for you. Many messengers hesitate to speak up because they worry that the situation cannot be controlled. Other phrases that are used to express this concern are: "Yes but . . ."

"I'm not really sure what the outcome will be."

"I can't be sure what she'll think or do once she hears what I have to say."

"He may come up with a different idea of what to do."

"I can't be sure that they'll accept my ideas."

"During the heat of the conversation I may not be able to think of the right thing to say."

If you have ever voiced concerns similar to these about a situation with a receiver, you are absolutely right. Once you bring the message out into the open and begin the dialogue, you cannot control what happens next. There are two reasons for this. First, your receiver is separate from you and will respond to you, your message, and your motivation in a unique way, based upon his or her thoughts, feelings, and values. Second, no matter how well prepared you are, you cannot have all the information or perspectives on the subject to be discussed. Your receiver's experience, insight, or observations will be different from your own. He or she may interpret a set of factors quite differently than you would. In your conversation, your receiver will probably reveal differences that may be a complete surprise to you.

The good news is that you *can* have a substantial influence on your discussion. You can do this by being clear about your true message and your real motivations. If you have carefully thought about how your receiver might respond, you can create a strategy that will help you to present your message in an effective way. Once the dialogue starts, you can influence the outcomes by using effective interpersonal communication skills, addressed in the Messenger's Tool Box. These influencing aspects are also covered at some length in other parts of this book. This information will be helpful if shifting from control to influence emerges as a compelling area of personal growth for you.

How to Understand Yes-Buts

Understanding yes-buts is not always easy. They are like dark clouds that never rain: present, noticeable, but with subtle impact. Once they have been identified, they are worth studying, paying particular attention to their impact. To do so:

1. Name your yes-buts.

2. Categorize your yes-buts as additional risks, excuses, or personal growth opportunities.

3. If they provide additional risks, review the assessment in Chapter Eight.

4. If they are excuses, balance them against the power of your motivation.

5. If they provide personal growth opportunities, develop a plan.

Figure 9.1 captures these steps, indicating that once the action needed to address a yes-but has been identified and categorized, it can lead in very different directions.

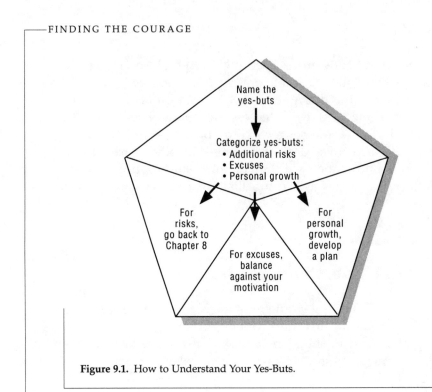

Figure 9.1. How to Understand Your Yes-Buts.

Step One: Name Your Yes-Buts

If you are still worried about bringing your message forward, this should be a relatively easy list for you to build, because yes-buts are seldom far from a person's consciousness. Again, by yourself or with a partner, answer the question, "What are all the reasons—other than the worries about repercussions that I have already identified—that keep me from going ahead with my message?" List as many as you can, using the opening line: "I'd like to speak up, but . . ." Here are Terri's yes-buts:

I don't know where the conversation with Richard will end up. Anything could happen!

This probably won't do any good. I've tried talking to him already and things have only gotten worse.

I may be wrong about this whole thing. After all, I am new and have less experience than Nellis. Maybe I should just back off.

Step Two: Categorize Your Yes-Buts

Review your yes-buts and decide whether each of them is an additional risk, an excuse, or a personal growth opportunity. This evaluation goes beneath the surface, to help you to better understand your hesitation about speaking up. In spirit, this clarification process is similar to the "Five Why's" exercise suggested in Chapter Seven as a means of understanding your real motivation. This simple line of self-questioning can reveal hidden aspects that are sometimes disguised with the phrase "Yes, but . . ." In Grid 9.1, Terri's yes-buts show how additional fears, personal growth opportunities, and excuses can be identified.

Step Three: If They Provide Additional Risks, Review the Assessment in Chapter Eight

If, like Terri, you identify an additional worry about a repercussion, return to Chapter Eight to assess how realistic that fear is. If it is realistic, balance it against the power of your message and your motivation by asking: "Are my reasons for speaking up important enough to outweigh this repercussion that is likely to happen?"

Step Four: If They Are Excuses, Balance Them Against the Power of Your Motivation

If you learn that you have excuses that stand in the way of presenting your message, it is time for you to consider the question: "Are my reasons for speaking up important enough to set aside my excuses and go forward with my message?" As Terri examined her yes-but related to the idea "It probably won't do any good," she realized that Richard had, in fact, taken action after her second meeting with him. It just wasn't action that she appreciated. As she thought about this excuse, it was clear that the benefits that might come from talking with Richard were far more important than this yes-but.

Yes-Buts	Risk, Excuse, or Personal Growth Opportunity
I don't know where the conversation with Richard will end up. Anything could happen!	*This is an additional risk. If Richard acknowledges that he has difficulty working with me, I'm afraid that I'll have to eventually leave, because if he doesn't like me, how can I be successful working for him?*
This probably won't do any good. I've tried talking to him already and things have only gotten worse.	*This is an excuse. I have to admit that Richard does take action. He finally did listen to my concerns about the audit; he took action, even though it was something I would not have chosen.*
I may be wrong about this whole thing. After all, I am new and have less experience than Nellis. Maybe I should just back off.	*This is an opportunity for personal growth. What's going on here is a long-standing pattern I have. When things get really tense, I tend to doubt myself, even when I've been very conscientious. I don't want to do that this time.*

Grid 9.1. Categorizing Your Yes-Buts.

If you find that you have trouble answering with a clear yes or no, consider these questions:

1. Does this excuse have as much influence over me now that I see it as an excuse?

2. What level of discomfort or disruption does this excuse protect me from?

3. Is that protection more important than achieving the benefits of bringing my message forward?

4. What will be lost if I don't speak up? How important is that to me?

Step Five: If They Provide Personal Growth, Develop a Plan

If an examination of your yes-buts reveals a thought or behavioral pattern that you would like to change, spend time developing a plan for doing this. You might want to:

- Ask those who know you well for their views on this pattern

- Keep journal notes that describe the circumstances when you see yourself thinking or behaving in this way

- Describe how you would like to see yourself behave or think in the future

- Identify the steps you will need to take in order to change this habit

- Set a timetable and identify people who can serve as supporters and resource people as you implement this plan

- Seek the guidance of a counselor or personal growth facilitator, if it would be useful, to help you to set goals and develop a plan that will minimize or eliminate this pattern

As she looked carefully at why she might want to cancel her meeting with Richard, Terri gained some helpful insights. She saw a pattern of discounting herself and her efforts. If she addressed this pattern and was successful, her efforts to understand her yes-buts would have payoffs well beyond the positive results of her discussions with Richard.

PERSONAL EXERCISES

Situation Exercise 9.1. Your Yes-Buts

Situation Exercise 9.2. Did the Process Work for You?

MAKE A DECISION

C HAPTER FIVE INTRO-
duced the notion
that, in order to find
the courage to speak up, messengers
need to embark on an inside journey of
personal reflection. In the four chapters
that followed, you were asked to look
inside yourself to answer a set of questions about your true message, real motivation, risks, and other reasons for not
speaking up. We encouraged you to go
deep, to look underneath your initial
responses in order to gain greater clarity.
In Chapters Eight and Nine you were

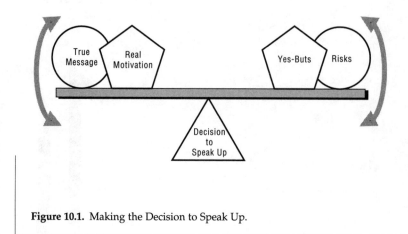

Figure 10.1. Making the Decision to Speak Up.

asked to balance the strength of your message and motivation against the risks and yes-buts that cause hesitation. This subjective and sensitive weighing process is reflected in Figure 10.1.

One step at a time, you have constructed a framework that has led to the current decision point. It is time to ask the question: "Are you going to speak up about your message or not?" The purpose of this chapter is to help you to make that decision and to be clear about the next steps to take—even if you decide not to deliver your message.

Options for Your Decision

Five options for messengers who are at this point are summarized in Grid 10.1. Look for the decision option and reasoning that best match your current point of view. When they are thought through, each decision is an honorable one. No precise formula exists to guide you in this type of decision making. The circumstances faced by messengers are too varied and are often highly personal. However, for each decision option, we'll suggest some key factors that, if they are present for you, might cause you to select that option. We'll also outline specific next steps that you might want to consider.

Decision Option	Reasoning Behind the Decision
Yes, I plan to go ahead.	The power of my message and motivation outweighs the risks and yes-buts.
Yes, and I need more time to get ready.	I need to develop a strategy and gather information to increase my chance of success.
I want to delay the decision.	I need more time to think about whether or not to go ahead.
No, but I will find another way to get my message across.	I realize that the risks are too great for me but that someone else might be able to be successful.
No, I will not bring this message forward.	The risks are too great for me to feel good about going ahead.

Grid 10.1. Decision Options.

"Yes, I Plan to Go Ahead"

Factors to Consider. When messengers decide to go ahead, they usually do so by focusing on the benefits rather than on the potential risks or their yes-buts. This means that the likelihood of repercussions taking place is relatively low or that the potential repercussions can be accepted in return for the benefits.

When the risk of repercussions is high, messengers who go ahead often are operating from a very strong value base. These messengers believe that they would experience high personal loss if they chose *not* to deliver the message. This might be a loss of credibility or personal integrity, or the potential benefits to the organization or others who are important to the messengers are so great that the messengers will face and take the risk. This

95

would be a classic case of speaking up because "it's the right thing to do."

Next Steps. If you decide to go ahead, continue reading. Both Part Three, "Acting with Courage," and Part Four, "The Tough Cases," provide practical advice for successfully delivering your message. The tips include specialized advice for handling the toughest of cases. Once your message has been delivered, Chapter Twenty will help you to debrief your experience, extracting the learnings that will enable you to improve the next time you decide to bring forward difficult news. Complete the Personal Exercises in Parts Three and Four, and review the communication skills material in the Messenger's Tool Box; it summarizes essential interpersonal skills that, when consciously applied, can greatly increase a messenger's likelihood of success.

"Yes, and I Need More Time to Get Ready"

Factors to Consider. For the messenger in this situation, the factors previously listed hold true as well. The difference here is that the messenger is probably a bit more nervous about how to actually deliver the message and respond to the receiver's comments. This messenger senses that to be successful she or he needs to do more careful preparation.

Next Steps. The remaining parts of this book, including the Personal Exercises and Basic Communication Skills in the Messenger's Tool Box, will be useful in developing a strategy. Other preparation might include thinking the issues through from the perspectives of others in the organization, including the receiver. In particular, you will want to:

- Think about the receiver's openness to feedback and to the specific message you plan to deliver

- Do relevant background reading and research or gather the useful opinions of others before delivering the message

■ Be clear about any time factors connected to your message, making sure that you do not take too long to prepare and lose the chance to deliver the message

"I Want to Delay the Decision"

Factors to Consider. Messengers who delay the decision tend to need more time to think about whether or not to deliver the message. Influencing factors can be:

■ Uncertainty about the likelihood of probable repercussions coming to pass

■ The belief that the benefits of speaking up are positive, but not compelling enough to inspire a clear willingness to take a risk

■ Unresolved yes-buts that the messenger is reluctant to give up in order to move forward

Next Steps. To help you decide whether or not to speak up, you might want to ask yourself these six questions:

1. What will be lost if I don't speak up?

2. How will I feel about myself if I don't speak up?

3. Does my hesitancy to speak up come from a hidden pattern of thinking or behaving that I need to resolve?

4. How long can I delay without losing the opportunity to speak up?

5. Is my delaying behavior a self-deluding tactic that allows me to avoid making a decision?

6. What would help me prepare to accept a higher level of risk at work?

Additionally, you might want to refer to the Personal Exercises, which will assist you in identifying your motivation, the potential risks involved, and the yes-buts that cause hesitation. If you have already done these exercises thoroughly, ask a trusted friend to help you to expand your thinking and to give you feedback about your decision-making process.

"No, But I Will Find Another Way to Get My Message Across"

Factors to Consider.   Messengers who arrive at this point usually recognize that the risks and yes-buts are significant and that the chances of their being successful are slim. Instead of just backing away, however, these messengers have a strong belief in the importance of their message. They understand that they are not the only ones who can play the messenger role. They are willing to do the work necessary to find someone else who can get the message through. The following risk factors identified in Chapter Eight are particularly relevant here:

- Is mistrust a noticeable element of your relationship with your receiver?

- Do you have a reputation as a troublemaker or a whiner?

- Are you different in some way from most of the others in your organization? Do these characteristics make communication more difficult?

- Have you been associated in the past with controversial issues that have a lingering negative impact?

Next Steps.   Take another look at the risk factors identified in Chapter Eight. As you read through them, think of your message and the people you know, or know of, who might be concerned about the same issues that prompted you to think about speaking up. Who among these individuals might face less risk than you in delivering your message to your receiver, or might be more likely to deliver your message successfully? You may ask others you trust and respect for their ideas about who might be an effective substitute messenger. Once you have decided whom you would like to deliver your message, approach that person with your request. If you don't know the person particularly well, it will be important to prepare carefully, to present yourself, your message, and your motivation in a compelling way.

If you find yourself tempted to use indirect or perhaps malicious methods to deliver your message, please reconsider. Anonymous notes, pointed cartoons mysteriously taped to the receiver's door, or abrasive E-mail messages are likely to backfire. For the receiver, such communications are confusing and often irritating. They provide the receiver with the sense that something is wrong, but without the opportunity to discuss the matter to find out more about the concerns.

Another option that might be available to you is the use of employee opinion surveys or suggestion box systems. If these are present in your organization and the timing is right to make them appropriate for your message, they might represent a safer way to get your message across. Be both reasonable and detailed in your comments so that your receiver will be able to understand what you want or need. The do's and don'ts presented in Part Three and Chapters Eighteen and Nineteen are useful for written messages as well as those delivered in person.

"No, I Will Not Bring This Message Forward"

Factors to Consider. If you have decided not to speak up, good for you! It takes courage to intelligently back away from a situation where the risk of repercussions to yourself or others is great or you need to work through other, longer-term issues first. This is particularly true in cases when one of the results of not speaking up is that you feel bad about yourself for not taking the risk. But no matter how you end up feeling about yourself, sometimes the risk is simply too big. Other reasons can also cause messengers to remain silent—for example:

- If they realize that their real motivation was to be hurtful to others or that they would be the only one to benefit from action taken on the message

- If they recognize that they are unable to bring forward a message that is honest, tactful, and nondefensive at the same time

- If they come to believe that, compared to all the other things the receiver is attending to, the message is not important enough to bring forward at this time

- If they realize that the message is not important enough to themselves to deliver at all

Next Steps. If you have reached this decision, consider continuing your exploration of this book. Future speaking-up situations may be close at hand and being prepared for them will always contribute to your chance of greater success. Reflect on your decision and the reasons why you decided not to go ahead with your message. Are there learnings about yourself or your work environment that may be useful in the future? Are there patterns about you or your organization that you find disturbing? If so, make note of them. In the future you may want to take action and the insight you have gained from reaching this "no" decision may come in handy. As you continue reading the next parts, you may want to select a new speaking-up situation to use as your personal case study, one where you have decided that speaking up is possible.

Moving Ahead with Courage

Finding the courage to speak up *is* an inside job. In Chapter Five we mentioned our friend whose vision quest really began as he explored his fears before he reached base camp. That came as a surprise to him because all his previous thoughts had been focused on the challenges that he would face during the three days of desert solitude.

Terri's experience reflects this pattern. Her thoughtful step-by-step preparation illuminated unanticipated aspects of her values, her experience in the organization, and her own behavior. Gaining clarity about these often-hidden inner dynamics helped to build her courage. It added to the strength that she gained by thoroughly understanding her message, her motivation, and the risks that she might face in talking with Richard.

This chapter points out that many options are available for moving ahead. Each is an honorable choice when it is made thoughtfully. As you go forward with your next steps, remember that you have already faced one of the toughest critics there is—yourself. If, in the last few chapters, you have challenged yourself with questions such as "Come on. Is that the real reason?" or "Why is that so important to me?" you are well on your way with the courageous messenger's journey. Prepared with new clarity and, perhaps, insight, you are now ready to bring your message forward.

*PERSONAL
EXERCISES*

Situation Exercise 10.1. How You Feel About Your Decision

Situation Exercise 10.2. Your Decision-Making Style

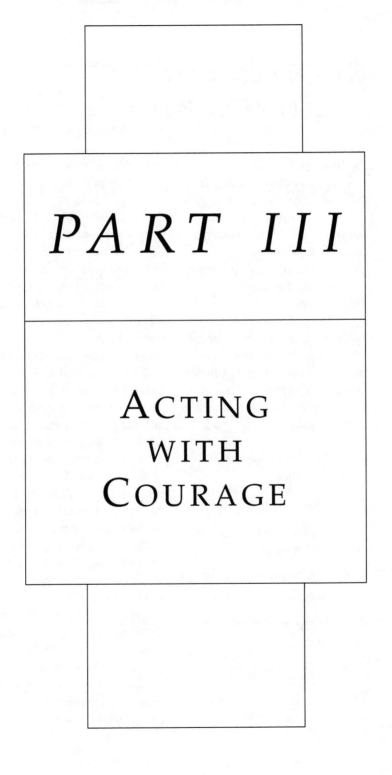

PART III

ACTING WITH COURAGE

STEPPING INTO THE UNKNOWN

You have decided to speak up. You are clear about *what* you want to say and *why* you want to say it. The next question is obvious: *How* do you say it so that your receiver is able to understand your message and is inspired to take action?

Helping you to answer this question is the purpose of the following six chapters. They are based upon the six phases in the conversation where you and your receiver talk about your message:

1. Get ready for the conversation.

2. Open the conversation.

3. Present your message and motivation.

4. Talk about your message with your receiver.

5. Wrap up the conversation.

6. Follow through.

Practical guidelines—do's and don'ts—are presented for each phase, and stories illustrate key points.

As you look at this list of steps, notice that particular emphasis is placed on the word *conversation*. Face-to-face conversations are the best way to make sure that messages are understood and to get the desired action from the receiver.

This type of interaction is not always possible, but it is the first choice for getting your message through successfully. As suggested in Chapter Two, speaking up is all about building and acting within constructive workplace relationships. Although technology and distance make it possible to communicate without face-to-face contact—or even make it necessary at times—most workplace interactions still take place between two people who are in the same place at the same time. The Messenger's Tool Box provides some useful suggestions for people who must rely on other types of communication.

It is this direct interpersonal contact that makes speaking up a risky activity. That's why this part of the book is called "Acting with Courage." Courage is required because you never know how things will go with your receiver. In the moment-to-moment interplay of a conversation, you cannot control how your receiver will react to you, your message, or how you deliver your message. The goal in this part is to help you to be successful in positively influencing this type of face-to-face encounter.

The chapters that follow will offer:

- ▨ A description of why each step is important

- ▨ A story that will serve as a reference point

- ▨ Tips for ways to successfully fulfill this step in your conversation

As we did in Part Two, "Finding the Courage," we encourage you to have a specific situation in mind where you have decided to speak up. It may well be the one you worked with in the previous chapters.

The stories offer a wide range of complexity and risk.

The situations and impacts described by the messengers touch on working relationships, personal behaviors, and work outcomes. Most, but not all, of the conversations are one-to-one situations in which a messenger brings a sensitive subject to a single receiver in a private setting. The messengers you will meet bring their concerns and ideas to their peers or supervisors.

These stories have been selected because they represent the most common everyday circumstances faced by messengers. In Part Four, "The Tough Cases," we build on what is shared in this part and offer specialized advice on handling the most difficult situations. These tough cases, which are similar in complexity and risk to the situation Sarah Eastland faced in the story in Chapter Two, rely on the same step-by-step process that is described here. If, in your reading of the next six chapters, your reaction is "When are they going to get to a really hard case?" remember that fundamentals that apply to the less complex situations are crucial when tackling a set of circumstances with higher risk.

GET READY
FOR THE
CONVERSATION

SUCCESSFUL MESSENGERS make the effort to get ready for their conversation with their receivers. The amount of preparation varies greatly. For some it can take a few days or a few weeks. Others may find themselves presented with an opportunity in the moment that they do not choose to pass up. In these cases, preparation may take place in a quick, quiet minute of reflection with a couple of notes scribbled on a pad.

Taking the time to get ready, regardless of the amount of time available, should be considered a conscious first step to bringing a message forward.

Why Getting Ready for the Conversation Is Important

When messengers unconsciously bring their issues forward, without thought about how to approach the receiver, they increase the chance that the potential risks involved will become real. However, when messengers carefully prepare, they position themselves to be successful, even with receivers who might be inclined to be defensive or resistant. This first step lays the groundwork for you so that the delivery of your message occurs with greater ease and effectiveness.

The better you know your receiver and her or his communication style, the better able you will be to set up a positive interaction. But even in cases where you do not know your receiver well, you can apply some general principles of respectful human relations to prepare for your conversation. Here is a story where the messenger and the receiver have worked together over a number of years. The situation the messenger is concerned about relates to the receiver's personal behavior, with a potential impact on work outcomes.

Tyrone's Story:
"They Don't Have the Quality We Need"

Tyrone works for a midwestern manufacturing company that has a contract to provide assembled components to another manufacturer. A quiet, steady person, Tyrone has worked for the company assembling components for eight years. A few years earlier, as a requirement for continuing to do business with the other manufacturer, his company began to implement a quality improvement effort. Involvement in various classes and two project teams taught Tyrone a lot about quality.

Three months ago, Tyrone's boss, Don, asked him to participate on a team that would recommend a single supplier for the machined parts they use in the components. Once he was involved on this investigative team, Tyrone's role was to collect data from the bidders to ensure that the supplier the company selected was committed to a program of continuous improvement. This would enable them to ensure delivery of quality parts to their own customer at an acceptable price. Tyrone's involvement seemed fairly straightforward until he realized that one of the final bidders on the contract was TZ Machine Shop. His company had done business with TZ for years. In fact, Don and the owner of TZ were personal friends.

Through his review of the bidders' quality programs, it became obvious to Tyrone that TZ Machine Shop did not have an effective effort to improve quality, especially compared to the other two bidders. It became equally clear that Don was pushing behind the scenes for TZ to get the contract. Tyrone knew that he would have to talk with Don about his concerns.

Tyrone decided that the sooner he shared his concerns with Don, the sooner the pressure he was feeling from him would be resolved, one way or another. Tyrone's analysis of the various bidders had prepared him with the information he would present to Don, but he took additional time to think through how he would phrase his concerns and what he hoped for from Don. He then asked Don for some time to discuss issues related to the bidding process. He deliberately set their meeting toward the end of the shift, knowing that Don's habit was to stay late to catch up on things. Tyrone knew that this would be a quiet time, with few others around to cause interruptions.

Tyrone began by thanking Don for asking him to be part of the team that would recommend the supplier. Tyrone added, "I recognize that you and the folks at TZ have known each other a long time. It's because of that relationship that I want to talk with you about something you may not be aware of." Curious, Don replied, "Oh, yeah? What's that?"

Knowing that Don didn't like long-drawn-out explanations, Tyrone got straight to his message. "I've read everything I could get my hands on related to TZ's quality efforts. I've come to the conclusion that they are not nearly as well designed as the other bidders. I don't think they can consistently deliver the goods we need. That's the opinion I'll be passing on to the rest of the team. I wanted you to know this in advance. I hope you will understand my reasons."

When Tyrone paused and took a breath, Don jumped into the conversation a bit defensively with "This is news to me. They've always done good work in the past. I'd like to see what you've based your opinion on." Having anticipated that Don would ask for this information, Tyrone gave him his folder.

109

Don read through the material and asked a number of questions. Tyrone answered them as best he could, staying focused on his need for Don to understand his concerns. He then added, "If we sign them up, I'm worried that we won't be able to deliver to our customer. That could mean we'd lose business—and, frankly, maybe I'd end up losing paid hours. In the last few weeks, I've been feeling a lot of pressure coming from you to support TZ's proposal. All of a sudden, it hit me that you might not know how they compare to the other bidders. That's why I'm here today."

They talked some more. Don asked specific questions about some of the other bidders. In the end, he looked at Tyrone and said, "You've done a good job on this analysis, Ty. I have to say I'm disappointed to see this, but you're right—on both counts. I didn't know this about TZ. I don't like hearing this, but I think you're right to go ahead with this recommendation."

MESSENGER TIPS   **Getting Ready for the Conversation**

Tyrone's approach to his conversation illustrates most of the do's and don'ts associated with this step of delivering a message.

Choose a good time and situation in which to deliver your message; do so as soon as possible. Don's personal relationship with the owner of TZ Machine Shop was well known. Once Tyrone realized that TZ did not have the necessary qualifications to be the successful bidder, he knew that he had a sensitive issue on his hands. Quickly, he set a time to talk with Don, making sure that they could do so in relative privacy.

Set up enough time to be able to fully discuss your message. Tyrone knew that a meeting at the end of a shift would provide enough open-ended time to discuss the issues that Don might put forward. When difficult news is delivered on the fly it can feel like a "dump-and-run." For the receiver, it can call into question the messenger's motives. Providing enough time to discuss the message sends a strong signal about your interest in a collaborative relationship and joint problem solving.

Spend time thinking about and preparing for your conversation.
Realizing that Don might interpret his message as a criticism of
his friend, Tyrone did not want to use words that would unnecessarily trigger any defensiveness, so he carefully thought about
both what he wanted to say and how he wanted to say it. It is a
good idea to consciously identify, then reexamine, the words or
phrases you plan to use to deliver your message. In your mind or
with a willing partner, role-play the conversation. Review the criteria outlined in Chapter Six. Ask yourself: "Am I constructing a
message that will be seen as honest, clear, direct, tactful, and
nondefensive?" Preparing these words ahead of time will
increase your confidence as you begin your conversation.

Take your receiver's communication style into consideration.
Can you detect a pattern in past conversations that should be
honored in this one? Preliminary talk about community events,
the weather, vacation activities, or the health of family members
can sometimes make it easier to get into the main points of your
message. Be open to the preferences of your receiver. A good rule
is to describe your motivation and share your message within ten
minutes of beginning your conversation. Because Tyrone knew
that Don understood the general purpose of their meeting and
did not like long explanations, he quickly presented his point. He
also brought along his information about the bidders and their
qualifications, anticipating that Don might want to see them.

*Be sensitive to how your receiver is likely to react to your mes-
sage, as well as to other things he or she might be facing at the
same time.* Two questions are useful when it comes to increasing your sensitivity to your receiver. First, will your message surprise or threaten your receiver or trigger an angry, defensive, or
hurt reaction? If so, why? Second, what else is going on in the
receiver's world that may make it hard for him or her to hear and
understand your message and motivation? If you know enough
about your receiver to answer these questions, you will be better
able to plan the timing and setting for your conversation. You
may also gain insight as to words or phrases to use, or avoid
using. If you feel that you do not have enough contact with your

receiver to answer these questions, try to imagine the circumstances faced by the receiver. Ask someone you trust who also knows your receiver for his or her impressions. This consideration shows your respect and empathy for the receiver.

Don't assume that your receiver cannot handle or is not interested in your message. Tyrone knew that Don was quite able to handle—and would want to know—his information. In some situations, however, this convenient yes-but can appear for messengers who have already decided not to speak up. On the surface, it might seem that the messenger is simply being considerate of the receiver by backing away from the decision to deliver the message. The reasoning often sounds like this: "I need to bring up what I've learned, *but . . .*"

> "He's so focused on other things right now that he won't be able to really hear what I have to say."

> "She'll be hurt by this news. It will send her into a complete tailspin. Better to put it off as long as possible."

> "I don't want to bother him with this right now. He doesn't need to be distracted."

> "It's not my place to tell her. This really ought to come from someone else."

As you discovered in Chapter Nine, such yes-buts can point to underlying and unidentified fears of the messenger. However, they are most frequently convenient excuses for not acting with courage. They can be demeaning to the messenger or the receiver—and sometimes both.

 PERSONAL EXERCISES

Story Exercise 11.1. Tyrone's Challenge

Situation Exercise 11.2. How You Want to Communicate

Situation Exercise 11.3. Your Receiver's Communication Style

OPEN
THE
CONVERSATION

IN THE LAST CHAPTER, Tyrone's story was used to illustrate the getting-ready phase of delivering a message. Here are some tips about how to open the conversation. This is the second step in delivering a message.

Why Opening the Conversation Is Important

As a conversation between two people gets started, both can feel discomfort. Sometimes "the tension is so thick you can cut it with a knife." *Effective messengers learn how to open conversations in a positive way that reduces this tension.* It is a step that gets the conversation off on the right foot, setting a constructive tone for the entire exchange. If the atmosphere is too tense, it will be hard for the receiver to concentrate on listening to the messenger. A skilled opening helps both parties to relax and be open to what is being said. The following story illustrates this point. It is a story in which the personal behavior of a new manager puts working relationships at risk.

 Angela's Story: "There's Something About Us You Probably Don't Know"

It was a Friday in the middle of December. Phillip, who had been on the job as vice president of the Employee Relations department for about six weeks, had arranged to take the members of his department to lunch. Everyone was looking forward to the event as a time to get to know each other better—including Angela, the director of organizational effectiveness. Little did she know that a simple lunch invitation would quickly turn into a situation where she would have to confront her new boss about his behavior.

Five years before, the company had changed its policy regarding the serving of alcoholic beverages at organization-sponsored social events. Prior to that time, as with many companies, alcohol had simply been a part of the organization's culture. Now that this was no longer the accepted practice, the members of the Employee Relations staff were very sensitive to the rumors they heard from time to time about how certain work groups did not follow the policy. The policy was well known, but obviously not everyone agreed with it. When it was not followed and an incident was reported, Employee Relations ended up dealing with the situation, so people in Phillip's new group were particularly careful to follow the practice themselves.

At lunch that day, when the waiter asked people for their drink orders, the first three people at the table ordered soft drinks. When the waiter came to Phillip, he ordered a glass of wine. No one said anything. The next person ordered iced tea. Then Steve, one of the managers in the group, ordered a beer. The rest of the group requested soft drinks. After lunch, back at the office, a significant buzz went around about Phillip ordering wine and Steve ordering a beer. People wanted to know what it meant. They were worried that their new boss might put their department in an embarrassing situation with the rest of the organization.

Fairly quickly, three people, including Phillip's secretary, made their way to Angela's office and asked her, "What will you do about this?" One of these individuals reported that she had confronted Steve by saying, "What were you doing? You know what department you're in!" Steve's reply had been a straightforward "Hey, I just followed the new boss's lead." Angela had already decided that she needed to say something to Phillip about the situation. The stakes for the department's reputation and the high level of energy that resulted from the situation at lunch made it clear that someone needed to take action. Because she was in a director's position and was a skilled communicator, Angela was the obvious messenger.

The question was how to get the conversation started. Looking back on the situation, Angela recalled, "This needed to be dealt with right away. If I had waited till Monday, the pressure would have been much greater. I took some time to think it through but didn't take too long." Angela waited until Phillip was free, then walked over to his office. Standing at his door, she said, "Phillip, do you have a few minutes? There's something that I think I need to share with you." His reply was "Sure. What is it?" Angela walked in, sat down, and continued: "Some things were going on at lunch today that I assume you don't know anything about. I thought it might be helpful if we had a chance to talk about them." She paused. With an open tone of voice, she continued, "Are you aware of the company's policy about alcoholic beverages?"

When Phillip answered, "No, actually, I guess I'm not," Angela was able to proceed with her message about his behavior, letting him know about the background on the issue and the unique role Employee Relations played in sorting out situations when the policy was not followed. In the end, he thanked her for the information, adding, "I thought something was strange, but I had no idea what it was."

| MESSENGER TIPS | Opening the Conversation

It is helpful to remember four key points when opening the conversation with your receiver. You will notice that these suggestions reinforce the tips we offered on getting ready for your conversation.

Express appreciation for the time to meet with the receiver and your hopes for a two-way exchange of ideas and viewpoints. In more formal situations, messengers frequently will set up an appointment to deliver their message. In those circumstances, a good way to open up the conversation is to thank the receiver for giving you the time to discuss your message. Angela dropped by informally; nonetheless, she specifically mentioned her hope of having a conversation about the problems at lunch by saying, "I thought it might be helpful if we had a chance to talk about them." When a messenger begins by expressing appreciation, talking about a hope, or making an offer, this tells the receiver that the messenger's attitude is constructive and respectful. From the receiver's point of view, it translates like this: "The news that's coming may be bad, but at least the messenger wants to help."

Open the conversation in a calm and tactful manner, quickly becoming more direct about your message. Angela said two things that were great examples of this suggestion:

> "Some things were going on at lunch today that I assume you don't know anything about."

> "Are you aware of the company's policy about alcoholic beverages?"

By saying these things, she was gently giving Phillip room to admit that he was not completely up to speed on company policy. Because he was new, this was an easy assumption for her to make. Her calm and open manner of saying so was diplomatic and set the stage for the message about his behavior. These two statements, along with her suggestion that talking about it might be helpful, enabled her to slide directly into her message.

Quickly entering into the heart of the conversation lets your receiver know that you have come for a serious purpose. Some other examples of ways you can open up a conversation include:

> "I observed something the other day that I thought you might want to know about. It pertains to _____. Is this a good time to talk?"

> "I know that you are concerned about _____. I have an idea I would like to share with you that might help out."

> "I've sensed that you really want to know what people think. I can offer some feedback that might be useful."

> "It occurred to me that you might not be aware that . . ."

These statements are valuable opening lines. They help you to start the conversation quickly and gracefully. Notice that if the messenger were to pause after any of the first three statements, it would give the receiver a chance to continue or stop the conversation. At a subtle level, this demonstrates respect for the receiver, and it does a lot to reduce the receiver's tension by giving her or him the opportunity to shape the conversation.

Have a sincere attitude and tone. The best way to approach your receiver is to do so sincerely, conveying a genuine concern about the issues you are raising. Sincerity is an important key to your credibility as a messenger. If you are genuine in how you communicate, you will make it easier for your receiver to listen to you. This is true even in cases where the receiver might instinctively disagree with your message.

It is hard to convey on paper the genuine quality Angela brought as she opened up her conversation with Phillip. And yet, because she really believed that Phillip had no idea that his glass of wine was a problem and would never consciously intend to go against a policy of that nature, she was able to be sincere. "Are you aware of the company's policy about alcoholic beverages?" is a question that, asked a certain way, could quickly put someone on the defensive. But because of Angela's sincerity about these concerns and her positive assumptions about Phillip, she was able to ask this question without triggering a defensive response.

Sincerity and conviction about the importance of an issue are very powerful communication devices. For most people, it's hard to fake being genuine. A manipulative or judgmental attitude usually inspires an unconscious use of words, phrases, or body language or a tone of voice that will suggest insincerity to the receiver. Honest and sincere communication often sounds quite unpolished or even awkward—far from perfect. When messengers set aside a desire to be perfect in how they present their message, they allow themselves the room to be real. This natural approach will tell the receiver that "this person is sincere. I should listen."

 PERSONAL EXERCISES

Story Exercise 12.1. Angela's Challenge

Story Exercise 12.2. What About Steve?

Situation Exercise 12.3. Know Your Opening Lines

PRESENT YOUR MESSAGE AND MOTIVATION

THE THIRD STEP IN A speaking-up conversation is presenting your message and your motivation for raising a difficult subject. If you have prepared for the conversation and have been successful in opening the dialogue with your receiver, the actual delivery of your message will be much less difficult than you might have originally imagined.

Why Presenting Your Message Is Important

When you present your message and motivation, you create a personal moment of truth. Presenting your message clearly, so that your receiver can understand your point, means that you have followed through on the commitment you made to yourself when you decided to speak up. Directly identifying your reasons for bringing your issues forward is equally important. As we have mentioned before, an unspoken motivation is easily misinterpreted—often from a negative slant. If you openly share your reasons for raising your concerns, your receiver will learn more about your message and the circumstances that make it important to you and will listen more carefully, because she or he will not be distracted by wondering whether you have some kind of hidden agenda. A receiver who listens attentively is much more likely to understand your point of view and be more willing to take action on your behalf. In the following story, which illustrates many of the do's and don'ts involved in this phase, the messenger brings forward a sensitive issue pertaining to work outcomes.

James's Story: "This Is the Wrong Product and the Wrong Partner"

James was a divisional vice president in a midsized telecommunications manufacturing company. He loved the fast pace and was proud to work for an organization where the business's strategy included "extending its global reach." Six months previously, at the beginning of a Korean project nicknamed Headlight, James was among the most enthusiastic proponents of the partnership. Then things changed and James's attitude about the project changed too.

When the Korean company had first approached his organization, James was all for the idea of expanding into the Asian market by partnering with this firm. Their proposal was thoughtfully presented and their general reputation was strong. While further discussions took place, James assigned several of his staff to more fully investigate the company and the market. As the information came in, James began to see the venture in a different light. At the project steering team meetings, he started asking pointed questions, some of which were never answered to his satisfaction. More than once, he received quizzical—and sometimes frustrated—looks from Eileen, his executive vice president. But he figured that he was hired to put his company's best interests ahead of his own, so he continued his investigation and his critical thinking.

When his staff had supplied him with enough information to cause him to believe that this was the wrong product with the wrong partner, he went to see Eileen. He shared the information with her, voicing his concern that the project looked good on the surface but held many hidden costs. His data suggested that the Korean company was not as credible as it had portrayed itself and the product was not right for the market at this time. "Please slow down," he said, "and take a closer look at all this." Eileen thanked him for coming and said she'd look into it. That was three weeks ago.

As he reviewed the agenda for today's project steering team meeting, it was clear to him that Eileen had no interest in backing away from the project. James realized that this meeting might be his last chance to press his concerns. Doing so in a more public arena was risky. In addition to Eileen and the rest of the steering team, his company's chief financial officer would be there. He knew that if his action embarrassed Eileen, his credibility would be at risk. In the worst case, it was not inconceivable that he'd be transferred to another division. He didn't think he'd get fired. He'd spent too many years and made too many contributions to the company's success for that to happen. Knowing the group and the players as he did, he spent time thinking about when and how he would raise his concerns.

Sure enough, the opening he was waiting for came when Karl brought up scheduling issues. With as positive a tone as he could find, James said, "Excuse me, Karl, but before we go any further, I'd like to reiterate some of the concerns I've voiced previously—problems that, no matter how much we talk, just do not seem to go away. I'm raising these issues again because I think it's important that our first expansion into the Asian market be a strong one."

He paused. No one said anything, but all eyes were on him. "You all know that six months ago, I was very enthusiastic about Headlight. Wanting to make sure we were on the right track, I started gathering information, which I've shared with all of you. I keep coming back to the same point: this is the wrong product and the wrong partner. Headlight will use time, money, and opportunity that could be invested elsewhere to more effectively extend our global reach. I worry that going through with this carries a high opportunity cost and will diminish our reputation in the Asian market in the long run."

Looking around, he saw a range of expressions, from passive to surprised to stony. He plunged ahead. "I have one request. Let's give ourselves two more weeks to rethink this. Let me bring in my staff to lay out what they've learned. You can grill them as long as you like."

Silence. Eileen, not surprisingly, was the first to speak. "Well, James, that was quite a speech. A cheap shot, if you ask me, since we've all looked at your worries before. In my view, you've been negative about Headlight from the very beginning. It's time for you to stop being a nay-sayer and get on board." She stopped and looked around the table. "I don't know what anybody else is thinking, but I'm ready to talk about scheduling." More silence. No direct eye contact between anyone. "Fine," she said. "Karl, where were we?"

The next afternoon, Bill, the company's CEO, dropped by James's office. What started out as a brief chat ended up in an hour-and-a-half meeting. At some point, Bill told James, "I heard about what happened at the steering team meeting. Eileen's committed to moving ahead with this and even though she was angry at you yesterday, she understands why you said what you did. I want you to know that I respect what you've done, but for political reasons we've got to go ahead. Will you be able to support it?" With the perspective that comes from a partial night's sleep, James was able to reply, "Bill, you're the CEO. I was doing what I thought was a part of my job. If you and Eileen and others think that it's right to move ahead, then you can count on me to support that decision." Reflecting some more, he continued, "I had to raise my concerns one more time. I hope you understand why." Later, as they parted, a warm handshake from Bill let James know that he had understood.

One year later, Headlight was abandoned due to a lack of response from the Asian market.

| MESSENGER TIPS | **Presenting Your Message and Motivation** |

In Part Two of the book, message and motivation were introduced. In Chapter Six, we suggested a formula for your message: a situation, specifically a problem, concern, or opportunity; the impact of the situation; and a request or suggestion for action. In Chapter Seven, we suggested that your motivation for speaking up stems from the reasons why you believe it is necessary to do so and the benefits that will come to yourself and others because of addressing your concerns.

James modeled several key do's and don'ts about presenting message and motivation when he spoke up to the project steering team. No particular sequence exists for bringing any of these points up during your conversation. What is important is that you share this information at some point in your dialogue.

Describe the problem or your concerns in terms that are important to the receiver. If you follow the formula we suggest, you will be able to connect your message to things that are important to your receiver. This happens when you identify the impact of the situation you are concerned about. James did this by linking his concerns about partnering with the Korean firm to the ability of the company "to extend our global reach." His message was: "If we pursue this relationship, it will have a negative impact on our ability to extend our global reach."

Essentially, this tip is based upon the notion of enlightened self-interest. When you are thinking about your message and how to present it to your receiver, ask yourself these questions:

"If my receiver does what I hope she will do, what benefits will come to her?"

"If my receiver does not do what I hope she will do, what negative impacts will occur?"

The better you know your receiver and the types of impact statements that most appeal to him or her, the more successful you will be. When you present your message in terms that are important to your receiver, you help him or her to remember—or perhaps discover—an aspect of self-interest that could be met by taking the action you are requesting. This provides the receiver with a reason to join you in addressing your concerns.

State clearly why you have raised your concerns and want to talk about them. A direct, sincere, and concise statement of your motivation clears up any confusion that may exist in your receiver's mind about why you have initiated this conversation.

James did this with his statement, "I'm raising these issues again because I think it's important that our first expansion into the Asian market be a strong one."

State clearly what you need, want, hope for, or expect from your receiver. At times messengers ask for clear, dramatic action from their receivers. In James's case, however, he simply asked that the steering team slow down for two weeks to reconsider its direction. The question you need to ask yourself is "What action do I want my receiver to take to address the concerns I am bringing forward?" Think in terms of *assertive statements*, short, concise statements like those that comprised James's request:

> "I have one request."

> "Let's give ourselves two more weeks to rethink this."

> "Let me bring in my staff to lay out what they've learned."

> "You can grill them as long as you like."

If you have trouble with this, return to Chapter Six and then consult the "Basic Communication Skills" section in the Messenger's Tool Box.

Don't whine, dump, or avoid responsibility; when you are involved in the problem, acknowledge your role. In discussions with receivers of tough messages, we asked, "What makes it hard for you to listen to a bad-news message?" In almost every case, the person we were talking to said, "Whining." You will be very likely to turn off your receiver if you:

- Present your message with a whiny tone
- "Dump" blame or criticism on another person
- Are unwilling to acknowledge your involvement in the problem (when that is the case)
- Cannot translate the problem into business results

This kind of behavior will convey the strong impression that your motives are confused or slippery. Your receiver may think you are trying to look good or get something at someone else's expense. If your behavior is having this effect, you may want to rethink your strategy for communicating with your receiver.

Don't overstate or exaggerate the problem by making insupportable or extreme comments; describe the factual impacts as accurately as you can. James did a nice job of sticking with the facts as he knew them and did not overstate them. He was prepared to bring in his staff to share their findings with the steering team.

Receivers of tough messages often find it easier to hear what the messenger has to say when it is conveyed in a calm tone and the issues are based on facts. A receiver who believes that you have exaggerated your concerns or asked for an action that seems like overkill may question your motives and judgment and lose interest in what you have to say. Additionally, the overstatement can raise the tension in the conversation because of the extreme feeling that an exaggeration can create.

Don't state your message or motivation in a voice that is too loud or too soft. A tip that goes along with keeping your presentation as factual as possible relates to the tone of your voice. Raising or lowering the pitch or volume of your voice adds a strong emotional context to your message. This sometimes happens unconsciously out of nervousness. You will help your voice seem more "natural" to your receiver if you:

- Speak slowly
- Remember to breathe
- Speak to one point at a time, then stop and listen to your receiver's reaction

Don't undermine the sincerity of your message and motivation through jokes, sarcasm, or innuendo. Bringing a tough message to a receiver is serious business. Messengers who have a quick sense of humor sometimes create problems for themselves when they try to break the tension of the moment. If you tell jokes, use

125

a sarcastic tone, or say one thing and imply another, you will risk confusing your receiver. This will make it harder for your receiver to focus on your message and trust your motivation.

Don't undermine the power of your message and motivation through self-deprecating remarks and apologies. It is also possible to undercut the power of your message and motivation by putting yourself down. Consider comments like the following:

> "Of course, this is just how I see it. Others may not think it's so important."

> "I know you have a million other more important things to do right now, but I sure would appreciate your help."

> "I could probably live with this situation . . . After all, I'm only one person who's being affected by this."

It is easy to see how a messenger might be tempted to use these and other similar statements to appeal to a receiver, by trying to make the receiver feel sorry for the messenger. Sometimes messengers use comments like these because they want to "be nice" to the receiver.

These approaches tend to backfire. Receivers can see such communication as manipulative or overly timid and, thus, a turnoff. Another understandable reaction can be: "Well, if the issues are so unimportant, why are you here talking to me about them?" Either way, the messenger diminishes his or her credibility and likelihood of success.

 PERSONAL
EXERCISES

Story Exercise 13.1. James's Challenge

Story Exercise 13.2. What About Eileen?

Situation Exercise 13.3. Your Receiver's Interests

Situation Exercise 13.4. Effective Request Statements

Situation Exercise 13.5. Say Your Message Out Loud

TALK ABOUT YOUR MESSAGE WITH YOUR RECEIVER

THE FOURTH STEP in the conversation with your receiver requires the most from you as the messenger. This most challenging aspect of the messenger experience is the work of dialogue and collaboration. It is by this means that you and your receiver gain new insight and understanding about each other's views and together reach some agreement about what to do next.

Why Talking About Your Message with Your Receiver Is Important

Given the complex nature of workplace relationships, it would be a rare situation for a messenger to present a message and have the receiver instantly understand the point and agree to take the requested action. It is the conversation that takes place after the message is delivered that helps the receiver to truly understand what the messenger is saying and why it is important. Without that understanding, it is unlikely that the receiver will be inclined to follow through with the action requested by the messenger.

The quality of this exchange often determines both the short-term and long-term results associated with being a messenger. This aspect of relationship building is illustrated in the next story, where the receiver's personal behavior had a strong negative impact on the working relationship.

 Betsy's Story: "I Would Appreciate It if You Wouldn't Talk Like That Around Me"

Betsy had finally reached the point where she could not stay silent any longer. One too many times, Lois casually—and probably unconsciously—had used the word *Jap* within earshot of Betsy. As a Japanese-American woman, Betsy found this language highly offensive, in a personal way. But it was more than that one word. Like a few others in their work area, Lois would make occasional derogatory comments about homosexuals. This also made Betsy uncomfortable, partly because she thought that some gay people might be on staff. She worried about how this made them feel.

Lois was a long-term employee. She and Betsy had met five years ago when Betsy came to work at the company's suburban warehouse. Betsy cared about keeping her relationship with Lois on a positive note, because to do her work well she needed Lois's cooperation. That's why she had pretended not to hear some of the things Lois said and made excuses for Lois's insensitive comments. "She's older," Betsy reasoned. "She doesn't understand the impact of her words. She would never intend to hurt my feelings." Additionally, Betsy had to admit that she didn't like conflict. Better to ignore unpleasant situations than to risk the possibility of their becoming worse.

Betsy spent a long time thinking about how to approach Lois. She didn't want to confront her in a public way. Lois had a quick sense of humor and loved an audience; she could easily turn Betsy's comments into a joke for others to laugh at. Betsy figured that it would not take too long for a situation to arise in which she would be able to raise her concerns.

Two weeks later, as she and Lois were on their way out of the coffee room, one of the men who worked in another area made a comment about the headlines concerning recent trade negotiations with Japan. He more than once used the term that was so offensive to Betsy. Later on that day, after she and Lois had finished going over some inventory figures, Betsy said, "Boy, Vincent sure seemed steamed up about the trade negotiations this morning! Does he always get carried away like that about politics?" "Oh, don't pay any attention to him," Lois responded. "He just likes to rattle people's chain early in the day. It's his way of having fun."

Recognizing the chance to introduce her message, Betsy said, "Well, you know, some of what he said really got to me." Lois quickly shot back, "I didn't realize you cared about politics." "That's not what I meant," Betsy said. "It was his use of the word *Jap.* That's a very hurtful word for me." Without missing a beat, Lois replied, "Well, if you're going to work here, kiddo, you've got to have a thick skin with people like Vincent around. He doesn't mean anything by it." Betsy took a deep breath and said, "Well, that may be true. But when he says words like that, I always feel put down. The same thing happens when you use that word. I feel like you're putting me down, even though I bet you don't mean to."

Lois stood still and looked straight at Betsy. "What do you mean?" Betsy responded, "I mean that it's important for me to have a good working relationship with you. I mean that you say things from time to time that make it sound as if you don't respect me. I want you to know that that way of talking hurts my feelings and gets in the way for me." Although she was uncomfortable, Betsy did not waver during the silence that followed. She waited. Finally, she said, "I want to believe that when you use words like *Jap* and *queer* and *colored,* you don't realize the pain they can cause for others. I would appreciate it if you wouldn't talk like that around me."

"Why haven't you said anything about this to me before now?" Lois demanded. "Because I was too shy. Because I was scared that you'd make a joke about it. I don't know. Maybe I didn't have the courage to say what I really felt." All the time Betsy was speaking, Lois kept staring at her, almost in disbelief. At last she said, with controlled anger in her voice, "So you're telling me that for the last two years you've had these reactions and have never said anything to me about them? Do you have any idea how that makes *me* feel?"

Betsy recognized that she had the chance to learn something about Lois. "You sound as if you're upset with me because I never told you that I was upset with you." "That's exactly right," Lois replied. "If you were unhappy working with me, you should have told me. That kind of talk is part of the world I grew up in. That's just the way I am, kid." Still listening, Betsy said, "So it never occurred to you that that kind of talk was hard on me." Pausing, Lois continued, "Well, it crossed my mind, but since no one said anything and some of the others around here use some of those words, I didn't worry about it much. Now that we're talking about it, though, I can see where it might make you mad."

As they gathered up their papers and prepared to leave the conference room, Lois reopened the conversation by saying, "Listen, you're a good kid. I like working with you. I'll try to be better about what I say, but I won't make a promise to be perfect." "I don't expect that," said Betsy. "All I ask is for you to see my point and try. I promise to let you know if you slip, okay?" "Okay. That's a deal," replied Lois as they walked out into the hallway.

| **MESSENGER TIPS** | **Talking About Your Message with Your Receiver** |

The dialogue between a messenger and a receiver requires that the messenger be particularly attentive to the receiver's verbal and nonverbal communication. The focus is on exchanging information, creating understanding, and building a relationship. Specific tips include the following.

Listen carefully to the receiver's perspective about your message, especially if she or he seems to resist what you are saying or becomes emotional. Once you have delivered your message and explained your motivation for speaking up, it is time for you to switch to a listening mode. If you keep talking in an attempt to persuade your receiver to see things your way, you will learn nothing of your receiver's initial reaction to your message.

Betsy paraphrased what she heard Lois say with "You sound as if you're upset with me because I never told you that I was upset with you." She learned more about Lois when she paraphrased again with "So it never occurred to you that that kind of talk was hard on me." Both of these statements encouraged Lois to tell her side of the story and gave Betsy an insight into Lois's reaction to her message.

If you can, offer additional information to help the receiver understand the importance of the issues to you. If you sense that your receiver is confused about what you are talking about or why you are bringing this message forward, sharing more information can be very useful. When you share this information, do so in a way that seems like an *offer* rather than a sell-job. To a receiver, the offer provides insight, whereas the sell-job puts on pressure. Some phrases that carry the "offering" spirit are:

"It was helpful for me to learn that . . ."

"One thing that might help you to better understand why this is important to me is . . ."

"After thinking about this, I also realized that . . ."

Don't make negative assumptions about your receiver's or others' intentions. This is a damaging pattern displayed by many messengers. Twice Betsy voiced her positive assumptions about Lois's intentions. Betsy said:

"I feel like you're putting me down, even though I bet you don't mean to."

"I want to believe that when you use words like *Jap* and *queer* and *colored,* you don't realize the pain they can cause for others."

When messengers make negative assumptions about their receivers' intentions, it is very difficult for this belief *not* to leak out through word choice, tone of voice, or body language. Once it is present in the conversation, this intangible aspect of the com-

131

munication immediately puts the receiver on the defensive because the receiver feels negatively judged as a person. And once the receiver is in a defensive posture, her or his willingness to listen openly or take action on behalf of the messenger becomes severely limited.

Although it is difficult to do so, it is possible for a messenger to give a very difficult message to a receiver about the receiver's behavior and *not* make a negative assumption about what the receiver intended to do. It is not necessary for the messenger to make a positive assumption the way that Betsy did. Simply staying neutral about the issue of the receiver's intention is a way to help maintain an open quality in the conversation. We cannot overemphasize the importance of this point.

Use neutral words to describe the behavior or circumstances that are creating problems, not phrases that communicate blame. A tone of blame is an extension of having made a negative assumption about a receiver's intention. This can only make it more difficult for a messenger to be heard and supported by the receiver. One way to prevent this pattern from occurring is to use neutral words to describe the behavior of the receiver. Look at Betsy's word choices, illustrated in Grid 14.1, to see the difference between neutral descriptive words and ones that are blaming.

Stay open-minded to what your receiver says; don't discount the receiver's reaction to your message or jump to conclusions based on your own biases. This tip is connected with the previous two. It requires messengers to know what their biases are and how those biases can influence interpersonal communication. It also requires messengers to consciously *not* allow those biases to unnecessarily influence their reaction to what the receiver says. This process of self-discovery can often be painful, but without the effort, it is easy for a messenger to unconsciously distort— and therefore discount—a receiver's response. This is especially so if the receiver has a defensive or resistant manner.

Given the circumstances, it might have been easy for Betsy to be biased against people who used derogatory slang or who seemed pushy in their communication style. As the story plays itself out, however, we see none of this. And as a result, we watch

Betsy's Neutral Descriptions	Betsy Could Have Been Blaming by Saying This
"It was his use of the word *Jap*. That's a very hurtful word to me."	"It was his *intentional* use of the word *Jap*. That's *obviously* a very hurtful word to me."
"But when he says words like that, I always feel put down."	"But when he says *bigoted* words like that, I always feel put down."
"The same thing happens when you use that word."	"The same *stupid and unnecessary* thing happens when you use that *awful* word."
"I mean that you say things from time to time that make it sound as if you don't respect me."	"I mean that you say *completely ignorant* things from time to time that *indicate to me* that *you are* a racist."

Grid 14.1. Neutral Descriptions Instead of Blame.

Betsy being open—rather than closed—to learning about Lois. When Lois responded to Betsy by saying, "Do you have any idea how that makes *me* feel?" Betsy saw something in Lois that she had not anticipated, something she could learn from. Lois wanted to talk about her feelings. Betsy paraphrased Lois and that response opened up the following insights about Lois:

- She did not want to hurt others or make them unhappy by her behavior.

- She grew up in a world where slurs were used to describe people who were different.

- She had previously considered that such comments might be hurtful but had set the thought aside because no one complained.

If Betsy's potential biases about Lois had interfered with her willingness to listen to and learn about Lois, these important aspects of Lois's character would have remained hidden. And the rich, more personal aspects of the conversation probably would not have happened.

If you find yourself getting emotional, describe your feelings rather than acting them out. If you find yourself getting emotional at any time during your conversation, it is wise to simply stop and acknowledge what is going on. Making a self-disclosing statement such as the ones below can help to break the tension and get you back on track. These statements can be about your message or what you are experiencing in the conversation. Describing your feelings is a great way to keep from acting them out. Here are some sample statements *related to a message:*

"I guess I'm angrier about this than I first thought."

"It's very hard to describe the amount of frustration I feel about all this."

"It makes me very sad to think about how all this has happened."

Here are some sample statements *related to the conversation:*

"I'm worried that you have not understood why I am here to talk about this."

"I get scared when you raise your voice and won't let me finish what I have to say."

"I'm confused about what to say. I can't seem to find the right words to express how I feel."

If you find yourself getting overly emotional at any time during your conversation, this is a solid clue that you may be in the midst of a tough case. If so, you might want to refer to Part Four, "The Tough Cases," for additional suggestions.

Look for opportunities to ask for feedback about your message or your manner of bringing it forward. If you sense that the *way* you outlined your concerns triggers confusion, defensiveness, or resistance in your receiver, ask for feedback. By asking for feedback on your delivery, you accomplish two important things: (1) you learn something that may be useful in the future and (2) you make it clear that your focus is on helping the receiver understand your concerns, not on expressing anger or blame. You also make it clear that you see this as an *exchange* of views, a dialogue in which you want to listen fully to your receiver. Here are some ways to ask for this information:

> "I realize I was pretty upset when I laid all this out a few minutes ago. Did that get in the way of your hearing what I had to say?"

> "I hope when I told you why I was here that you didn't get the impression that I was trying to blame you for what's gone on. I'd like to know your reaction."

> "This is hard stuff for me to bring up. Did I present it in a way that let you understand what I was trying to say?"

> "When I'm nervous, I'm not very good with words. If you have some ideas about how I could have said all this so it would have been easier for you, I'd really like to hear them."

Each of these examples has the messenger offering some type of self-observation about how the message was presented. This acknowledgment of less-than-perfect delivery is a way to share your feelings about what is going on. Describing how you see your delivery and asking for feedback introduces some of your own vulnerability into the conversation. This very human gesture often helps a receiver to relax and be more open.

If it is appropriate, discuss what you are willing to do or what you have already been doing to deal with the situation. Betsy provided a good example of this suggestion. She said to Lois, "All I ask is for you to see my point and try. I promise to let you know if you slip, okay?" In this way, she made an offer of what she was willing to do to support Lois as she tried to change her behavior. When it is possible—and appropriate—for a messenger to offer such assistance, it can do a lot to reduce the emotional distance between a messenger and a receiver. It can also provide practical help, which can result in a greater chance that the messenger will get the desired action from the receiver. In situations where a messenger brings forward a message that is task-focused, it is particularly useful if he or she can describe what has already been done to improve things or keep them on track.

If possible, offer ideas about what to do next. As part of your message, you will suggest or ask that your receiver take some kind of action. This request can be useful to your receiver, but a question often remains: How does the receiver get started doing what needs to be done? Sometimes messengers can make the mistake of assuming that if the receiver understands the point and agrees to help, she or he will know what to do. The receiver may need ideas from the messenger to know what to do next.

PERSONAL EXERCISES

Story Exercise 14.1. Betsy's Challenge

Situation Exercise 14.2. Asking for Feedback from Your Receiver

Situation Exercise 14.3. Know Your Assumptions

WRAP UP THE CONVERSATION

YOU'VE DELIVERED YOUR message and your motivation. You and your receiver have spent time talking about your concerns, what you would like your receiver to do, and the receiver's reaction to what you have presented. "What else is there to do?" you may be wondering. Although the most demanding part of the conversation may be over, an important last piece remains. This step has to do with closing the conversation in a way that does two things:

1. It summarizes the understandings reached and the agreements made for the next steps.

2. It concludes the conversation as graciously as possible.

In this chapter, we will explore the details of this last aspect of your conversation.

Why Wrapping Up the Conversation Is Important

This step enables you to make sure that you understand—as much as is possible—what happened during the conversation. It reinforces any understandings or commitments that have been reached, therefore making it more likely that things will change as a result of your bringing your message forward. If the conversation was difficult, it allows you to acknowledge the emotional side of the conversation and any insight you may have gained about the receiver or yourself. It also gives you a chance to express appreciation or apologize, if need be. All of these actions can be a means of building a longer-term and more positive relationship with your receiver.

Neglecting these finishing touches can undermine the potential success of the messenger, as the following story illustrates. In this story, the personal behavior of the receivers has a negative impact on the working relationship.

 Adam's Story:
"Please Help Me Succeed!"

Adam and some of the other sales representatives were troubled by the same thing. Finally, when they compared experiences one evening over beers, it was pretty clear. Karen and Peter, the sales manager and the assistant manager, were not doing what they had promised. They were not spending sufficient time with the new reps in field training.

When Adam and his co-workers came into the organization, a direct mail company based in the Southeast, they were promised "hands-on, practical training" by "those who had been there and been successful." That meant Karen and Peter. The people who gathered that evening after work admitted that they felt left out of the attention that some of the other sales groups in other regions seemed to be receiving. Some worried about their ability to meet their quotas without more coaching. After all, it was very competitive out there.

When Adam joined the company, Karen had made her position clear in her one-to-one welcoming discussion. "If you want help, all you have to do is ask," she had said. An enthusiastic and assertive young man, Adam saw that he had a lot to learn and he believed that both Karen and Peter had the kind of experience he would benefit from. It scared him a bit to think of a manager observing him on an actual sales call and then critiquing his performance, yet he knew that this was exactly what he needed in order to improve and succeed in the long haul. Adam knew that Karen and Peter were very busy and had a lot of extended responsibilities, given a recent merger. He told himself, "They're probably just waiting to see if we've got enough initiative to ask." Adam had been in the organization long enough to know that in spite of the complaints of his co-workers, no one had ever directly asked for more training.

Adam had no reason to doubt the sincerity of Karen's initial offer, so he scheduled an appointment with Karen and Peter at the same time. He wanted to meet with them both to let them know his interest and to work out a training plan. The day of their meeting, Adam was a bit nervous, but he moved ahead. He was the leading sales rep in his group and he figured that they knew it was in their best interest to help him succeed. He described his concerns. He told them that he liked his job, but that it was stressful. He knew that having them go out on calls with him would be more stressful, but that was what he needed to do to improve. He was ready to take them up on Karen's offer. During the conversation, both Karen and Peter were receptive to Adam's concerns. The interaction moved along fairly easily and, at the end, they seemed ready to respond to Adam's request. Thanks were expressed all around for the opportunity to talk through these kinds of issues.

Adam continued to do his best. Neither Karen nor Peter went out into the field with him. He placed calls and left messages reminding them of their promise. His frustration in the field and his disappointment about his leaders quickly added up. Within two months of his speaking-up conversation, he had decided that this was not the organization for him and left to find opportunities someplace else.

Looking back on it, Adam found that he had learned a lot. He said, "I would have tried to think things through better before the meeting, in terms of what I wanted and how I would ask for it. I would have pushed more during the meeting for them to 'walk their talk' about mentoring and coaching. I would have been clearer regarding follow-up, including contracting for dates to do what they had agreed to do." In the end, Adam felt that his behavior had contributed to the end result, which was that he did not get what he wanted. This happened, in part, because he did not push for clear agreements about how Karen and Peter would provide the training he needed. When they did not follow through, he had no specific commitments he could use to focus their attention on his concerns.

| MESSENGER TIPS | **Wrapping Up the Conversation** |

Adam's story underscores the practical importance of consciously wrapping up the conversation. It is an easy step to overlook. When it is ignored, it can have a big impact on what a messenger might experience. In wrapping up, two aspects deserve attention: (1) the need for action planning and (2) the need to attend to the relationship between the messenger and the receiver. Here are some do's and don'ts that pertain to both of these points.

Summarize understandings, agreements, and any commitments for action. A summary lets everyone involved know what to expect of each other and encourages action when the conversation ends. If time frames or schedules are important, make sure that the dates are clear.

Depending on the complexity of the message and the need for follow-up, consider taking written notes that document a plan of action. These can serve as a record of your mutual decisions. Introduce this idea to your receiver when you are talking about what to do next. At that point you can say something like "This is getting pretty detailed. If you don't mind, I'd like to take some notes about what we are saying we'll do. I'd be happy to make a copy for you when we're done."

What	Who	When
Share the schedule of upcoming sales appointments with Karen and Peter.	Adam	By the end of business today
Identify two days each in the next month to spend with Adam.	Karen and Peter	By Wednesday (list the date)
Identify the aspects where coaching would be most helpful.	Adam	By the end of next week (list the date)
Meet individually with Peter and Karen to review coaching areas and seek general advice on sales techniques prior to going out in the field together.	Adam	Set appointments by Friday (list the date)

Grid 15.1. What, Who, and When.

Once you've completed your notes, simply make a copy of them so that both you and your receiver have a written reminder of what agreements you have made. An easy-to-use format is displayed in Grid 15.1. To illustrate how it is used, we've filled it out in retrospect, based upon what Adam might have done in his conversation with Karen and Peter.

There are two cautions. First, if you take notes on your agreements, it is important to do so in a way that feels helpful, rather than controlling. The *way* in which you suggest that you'd like to take notes will make a big difference. For example, you would probably not want to say something like "I'd like to take some notes to make sure there is follow-through *this* time."

A comment like this can easily be misinterpreted as an attempt to control the situation. It implies a negative assumption about the receiver's interest in taking action. Receivers who sense this may think that you want to set up a chance to blame them later if they don't carry out their end of the plan. This will dampen any enthusiasm they may have for following through, accomplishing the exact opposite of what you intend.

The second caution is that people vary not only in their communication style but also in their approaches to problem solving or planning. Some people are not comfortable about committing to a specific plan of action in the moment. If your receiver is such a person, you may sense resistance if you try to get too concrete about the next steps.

If this happens, you can do two things. The easiest is to use paraphrases, clarifying questions, and assertive statements to reach a general understanding of what will happen next, making sure that it is not so vague that it has no meaning. The second option is to ask about the resistance you sense. Your receiver may be worried about something related to the next steps or see a problem that he or she has not voiced to you. This option relies on your ability to make neutral observations and self-disclosing statements. Here are some ways to open up that possibility:

> "I get the feeling that you might not commit to anything too specific at this point. Is there some problem you see?"

> "I'm feeling good about jotting down some agreements. Are you okay with that? Is there something else we need to talk about? I don't want you to feel pushed."

Reinforce your reason for bringing your message forward. This is particularly important in conversations where you may have sensed resistance. Since a messenger's motivation can easily be misinterpreted, it is a good idea to reinforce why you have come forward. If you want to be able to continue to bring up tough issues with your receiver when they arise, talk about the relationship-building aspect of your motivation. Here are some examples of how Adam could have expressed his thoughts:

> "Before we leave, I want to reinforce my reasons for bringing this up. I'm excited about this job and this company. I want to do well, because that will be good for us all."

"I hope you understand why this conversation has been important to me. I'm not trying to make your lives more complicated. I'm here because I want to do my best but feel I need more coaching to do so."

"I hope you don't think that I've come here today to suggest that you haven't been helpful. I'm here because I wanted to take you up on your offer, and I figured you needed to know that I was interested."

If the conversation was difficult, acknowledge the emotional side of what happened. If the conversation was tense, it is a good idea to say something about it. This can help to repair any leftover negative feelings that might still be in the air. Offering your thoughts about your learnings, insights, or observations about the conversation can do the same thing. Two possible circumstances should be considered. Here are some examples when *the conversation was difficult, but got better:*

"I don't know about you, but until we discussed how our experiences were so different, I was getting pretty uptight about where this was going."

"I appreciate your willingness to stick with our conversation until I was able to be clearer about my concerns. I could see that you were upset with me for a while."

Here are some other examples, when *the conversation stayed difficult throughout:*

"I know this was very difficult to hear. It was also difficult to say. I hope we can continue this conversation after each of us has had a chance to cool down."

"Though we obviously have strongly opposing views, I've gained an important insight into why you do what you do. That helps."

End the conversation graciously. Conclude your conversation with a sincere thank-you for the receiver's time and attention.

143

Simple guidelines of courtesy suggest that some kind of appreciation for the receiver's effort is appropriate. The ending of your conversation can reinforce your commitment to follow through on any agreements that were made. These small aspects of your exchange contribute to building a positive ongoing relationship with your receiver. Adam's conversation might include the following expressions of thanks:

> "Peter and Karen, I want to thank you for meeting with me. I know you both have busy schedules. It means a lot to me that you were willing to take the time to listen."

> "I really appreciate this conversation. Thank you. Even though I know I'll be nervous at the time, I look forward to having you go out on sales calls with me."

> "This has been great. I'll get back to you about what my schedule looks like for the next month. Thanks again."

These points may seem small, but they are a way to ensure that a friendly, cooperative spirit is reflected in the last words of your interaction.

 PERSONAL EXERCISES

Story Exercise 15.1. Adam's Challenge

Story Exercise 15.2. What About Karen and Peter?

Situation Exercise 15.3. Moving the Conversation Toward Agreements

Situation Exercise 15.4. Imagining Your Follow-Up Agreements

FOLLOW THROUGH

THE LAST STEP IN acting with courage comes when you follow through on the commitments made with your receiver. Here the goal is to implement the planned actions while reinforcing the relationship.

Why Following Through Is Important

When you and your receiver do what you have agreed to do, it is a sign that both of you are serious about wanting to make changes and take constructive action. In turn, this can create a higher level of trust and respect. These two ingredients are essential building blocks for positive, ongoing working relationships.

To experience these changes and their benefits, you must hold up your end of the bargain by following through on your commitments. Sometimes, however, your receiver does not or cannot follow through as planned. This situation may require you to have another conversation with your receiver. The next story reflects a difficult situation in which the receiver does not keep her agreements, forcing the messenger to speak up again. Here, the receiver's personal behavior has a negative impact on work outcomes and the working relationship.

 *Benito's Story:
"We've Got to Talk"*

Leaving Cindy's apartment, it was hard for Benito not to jump to some negative conclusions about Pam. But he had promised that he would not do that and he was determined to keep up his end of the bargain. Yet it was obvious that he and Pam needed to talk more about her interaction with Cindy. As he drove back to their office, he mentally prepared himself for what he thought might turn out to be a messy conversation.

Benito and Pam were involved in a joint agency project called Look Ahead. The focus was on keeping inner-city teenage mothers in school and encouraging them to maintain proper nutrition and health care during pregnancy and through the first year of their baby's life. Benito was a case worker, working with parenting, family dynamics, and socioeconomic and school issues. Pam was a public health nurse, addressing nutrition and health care for both the baby and the mother. Benito and Pam had been assigned to work on a case involving Cindy and her baby, Celina.

Within a month's time, it became clear that the baby was underweight. When Benito made this observation and talked with Cindy about the baby's feeding schedule, he learned that Pam had not advised Cindy properly about the amount of formula her baby should have each day. Benito immediately talked with Pam about his concerns. In the conversation that followed, Pam said that she was operating on years of experience and thought that in this baby's case, slightly less than the standard recommended amount was correct. Benito took a risk by asking if Pam's personal eating habits (she appeared to suffer from anorexia) might be negatively affecting her judgment in this case. She rejected and resented this question.

Benito offered to arrange a consultation from the nutritionist who was available to their program. Pam admitted that this might be a good idea and agreed to follow the nutritionist's advice. At the end of their conversation, Benito felt that he had been too personal in his remarks about Pam's eating habits. He said that, in the future, he would not jump to conclusions about the reasons behind Pam's professional decisions without first presenting his concerns to her. She thanked him for that commitment. And so ended Benito's first speaking-up conversation with Pam.

It was no surprise to Benito that when the two of them met with the nutritionist, the standard feeding practice for babies of Celina's age and weight was reinforced. Pam said that she would share that information with Cindy. The next week, when Benito made his regular visit, he found that Cindy had no knowledge of the plan that Pam was to have shared. Apparently, Pam had gotten a phone call during her visit with Cindy and left shortly thereafter. Benito took extra time that day to give Cindy the full information she needed about the proper amount of formula for her baby. In order not to alarm Cindy, Benito stretched the truth a bit by explaining that he and Pam had recently received new information, which was why this advice was different from what Pam had told her.

Fortunately, Pam was still in the office. "I've just come from Cindy's. We've got to talk," Benito announced as he paused at her open door. "What if I come back in about fifteen minutes?" Pam looked hassled. "Fine," she said. "That will give me time to finish what I'm working on." Benito was aware that he was angry, but he tried hard to stay open-minded. He understood enough to know that if he came on too strong with Pam, nothing would get resolved. That fifteen minutes would give him a chance to focus on what he needed to find out. "And maybe it will give her a chance to think about this mess before we get into it," he thought to himself.

147

When Benito sat down in the chair next to Pam's desk, she was quick to say, "How's Cindy doing with Celina today?" Choosing his words carefully, Benito said, "Celina's weight is still down. When Cindy told me that you hadn't said anything about the new feeding plan, I filled her in on the correct amount of formula. I told her that we had consulted with a nutritionist and that he had given us new information. I didn't want her to think that you and I didn't have our act together. That wouldn't have done her any good."

"Thank you. You were good to say that to her," Pam said warmly. Benito paused, then added, "Cindy said that when you were there on Friday, you got a call and had to leave quickly. I hope that was the reason why you didn't pass on the information about increasing Celina's formula." He paused again. "Because if it wasn't, we need to talk about your willingness to follow through on your commitments with our clients. As you can probably tell, I'm very worried about this."

"Benito, if I were in your shoes, I'd be upset with me. The phone call was from my daughter's school. She was sick and needed to be picked up right away. At the time it sounded serious. I was distracted and completely forgot about the feeding plan." A bit surprised, Benito could only say, "How is she now?" Pam smiled, "Oh, she's fine. Just a nasty twenty-four-hour bug."

Frustrated, Benito shifted the subject back to Cindy and Celina. "Pam, I appreciate how your concern for Molly sidetracked you. But today is Wednesday. It's been five days since you saw Cindy. That's five additional days that this underweight infant was not receiving the proper nutrition. Why didn't you call Cindy about this? Or why didn't you call me and have me take care of it sooner?"

"I honestly don't know," was all that Pam could say. With tears starting to well up, she went on. "I do know that I've thought a lot about what you said about my own eating habits clouding my professional judgment. I'd hate to think that was the case, but you may be right. This last couple of months have been very difficult for me." Seeing an opportunity to get some more insight into Pam, Benito responded with "So it sounds as if there's more going on than this stressful job." "That's right," Pam said. "Although I think the job is most of it."

Benito wanted to be supportive of Pam but did not want to get side-tracked. Allowing some time for her last comment to rest, in a quiet voice he suggested, "It seems to me that there are two issues here—one that has to do with your work and one that has to do with you. I'd be glad do whatever I can to support you, Pam, in working on your personal issues. Just let me know. But whatever happens on that, you and I *must* reach some kind of agreement about how we'll work with Cindy and Celina. They need the best that we can give." With a choked voice, Pam said, "I know they do. But I feel so confused about everything, I don't know what to say to you."

Recognizing that this was not the time to push for much of anything, Benito decided to back off. "Okay," he said. "How about this? Let's get back together tomorrow after the staff meeting to continue this conversation. I don't want to let this go, but I can see that you need a break for today." "I'd appreciate that," Pam replied. Benito reached over and gave her hand a supportive squeeze. "We've all been in tough places, Pam. It's hard enough with normal jobs, but in this line of work, it can really pile up. We'll talk some more tomorrow."

| MESSENGER TIPS | **Following Through**

The do's and don'ts given here focus on ways to follow up on the commitments you and your receiver made at the close of your conversation. In addition, we offer some ways of handling sticky situations like the one Benito faced.

Make sure that you do what you told your receiver you would do. If timing is important, be prompt with your actions. Remember that your receiver may not be able to take a certain action until you do. When you've followed through with your agreements, report back to your receiver on what you've done or might have learned. In Benito's two-conversation story, he followed through quickly in arranging to meet with Pam and the nutritionist. In this circumstance, timing was critical because of the risk faced by an underfed infant. Although it was less visible to Pam, he also worked hard to honor his commitment to not jump to conclusions about Pam's decisions or actions.

Stay practical and flexible; recognize that your plans may need to change or be renegotiated as other events take place. When Benito recognized that Pam had not conveyed the feeding plan to Cindy, he was willing to take on some of Pam's area of responsibility. The baby needed more formula than she was getting and he could not wait any longer for Pam to deliver the information. Similarly, in his upcoming conversation with Pam, he needed to stay focused, positive, and practical. Heading into his second conversation with Pam, he had several questions on his mind:

- Was the phone call that cut short Pam's visit with Cindy a valid reason for not sharing the feeding plan?

- Why hadn't she gotten back to Cindy since that meeting?

- In her future interaction with Cindy, was Pam going to support recommended nutritional practices?

- If not, how would Benito make this happen?

- If not, what was Benito's responsibility to Cindy? to Pam? to Look Ahead?

- Would these circumstances lead to a change in his role in this case? If so, what might that be?

- Would Pam be upset with him for bringing this situation up again? Would she think he was unfairly jumping to conclusions about her intentions or competence? Would that cause her to do things that might represent a payback to Benito?

Benito recognized that he could not know the answer to any of these questions until he met with Pam, and therefore he needed to stay open-minded. His priorities were to get Celina fed properly, to make sure that Cindy and her baby received the full benefit of Look Ahead, and, finally, to keep any miscommunication or interpersonal conflict with Pam from interfering with that overall commitment.

In his second conversation with Pam, Benito found that she was going through a hard time personally. Her expressions of vulnerability and confusion required Benito to shift into a semi-counseling role—something he probably had not anticipated as he prepared for this conversation. Although he was able to be flexible on that point, he did not back away from delivering another message to Pam about keeping her commitments.

If your receiver promised to do things and you believe that this has not happened, voice your concerns. To do this, Benito first summarized to Pam what he had learned from Cindy. Then, in regard to the unexpected phone call during Pam's last visit, he said, "I hope that was the reason why you didn't pass on the information about increasing Celina's formula." He continued with "Because if it wasn't, we need to talk about your willingness to follow through on your commitments with our clients. As you can probably tell, I'm very worried about this."

In these lines, Benito relied primarily on assertive and self-disclosing statements about his feelings. He chose neutral words that were accurate for his feelings and less likely to trigger defensiveness on Pam's part. His tone was respectful of her, and he did not pass judgments or make assumptions about what was behind her behavior. These are all wise tips to remember when you find yourself in this type of situation. Here are other phrases you might use in a situation like this:

> "I'm concerned that you haven't been able to take care of the items you said you would do. Can I help?"

> "If we don't follow through with what we said, I'm afraid our efforts will be wasted. Has something changed for you that makes it hard for you to go ahead?"

> "It looks as if things have gotten bogged down on your end. I'd like to know what's happening from your point of view."

Notice that in each of these suggestions, the statement of concern is followed by a request for conversation or an offer to help. Both of these indicate that you are staying positive and want the action to move forward in a collaborative way.

If you still get no response—or you get defensiveness or open resistance—you probably are in the middle of a tough case. Your receiver may have hidden reasons for the lack of follow-through that she or he cannot or will not share with you. Or the two of you may be approaching the situation from different and incompatible views that surface only when it comes time to act.

151

These aspects are addressed in Part Four, which focuses on handling tough cases. In particular, you may want to look at the advice offered in Chapter Nineteen that describes the way a third party can be used to resolve a situation such as this.

If your receiver does not follow through, don't make negative assumptions about his or her intentions or jump to conclusions about why the expected action did not take place. As you can see from examining some of Benito's comments, he did a good job of not jumping to conclusions about Pam when she did not follow through. In particular, in a second conversation focused on a lack of follow-up, it is helpful to assume a collaborative attitude. After all, you made agreements once. The reason you are having a second conversation is that you care about the issues and want the receiver to be successful at keeping his or her commitments. Making negative assumptions about your receiver's intentions breaks this collaborative approach. It will only distance you from your receiver and decrease the likelihood that the action you desire will take place.

 PERSONAL EXERCISES

Story Exercise 16.1. Benito's Challenge

Situation Exercise 16.2. Your Own Follow-Through

Situation Exercise 16.3. Staying Flexible

Situation Exercise 16.4. Planning a Second Message

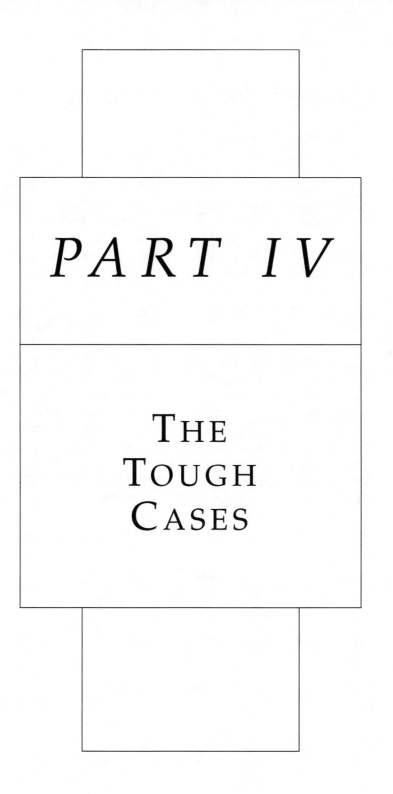

PART IV

THE
TOUGH
CASES

SOMETHING SOLID TO STAND ON

Some speaking-up situations demand more from a messenger than others. These are the *tough cases*, situations that for a variety of reasons require something beyond what is needed in an everyday act of courage. Tough cases are tough because they carry with them a greater risk that things will go wrong and that some kind of calamity will result. These cases require, therefore, greater energy, skill, and self-acceptance from the messenger. Because of this, a special part—a sequel to Part Three—has been added to assist you with these challenging cases.

Some readers will most likely turn first to these chapters because they are facing a tough case and are hoping that a "silver bullet" will be found within these pages to deal with the situation. You will find help here, although finding a single simple technique is not realistic for situations as complex as these. Carefully building on the tips presented in Part Three, these chapters offer criteria that will help you to determine when you are facing a tough case and additional advice for handling these most difficult situations.

DO YOU HAVE A TOUGH CASE?

TOUGH CASES CARRY the greatest threat to the receiver and the greatest risk to the messenger. In these situations, the repercussions that you identified when you made the decision to speak up are much more likely to come true than in other circumstances.

What Makes a Tough Case?

Three major dimensions can be involved in making a situation particularly risky. Any one of them can do it, and sometimes all three may be present. They have to do with the messenger's *perceptions of difficulty or threat* related to:

1. The receiver's character or personality

2. The dynamics between the messenger and the receiver

3. How difficult it will be for the receiver to hear the message and the messenger to send it

Perceptions About the Receiver

The receiver might be anybody: a manager, co-worker, or employee. He or she might even be a customer. Regardless of who the receiver is, the messenger mistrusts the receiver's character or personality. Among other characteristics, the receiver may be viewed as:

- Vindictive and controlling
- Highly emotional, taking things personally and getting very angry or upset as a result
- Clever and manipulative
- Someone who politely listens or makes promises but never seems to take action

Perceptions About the Dynamics Between the Messenger and the Receiver

These perceptions of the receiver create a background feeling of mistrust. For whatever reasons, the messenger does not trust the receiver. As a result, the messenger:

- Finds it very difficult *not* to make negative assumptions about the receiver's intentions

- Disagrees with the receiver about key values, which causes the messenger to judge the receiver as "wrong" in his or her views, attitudes, or behaviors

- Gets engaged emotionally by *both* the receiver's behavior and his or her potential behavior

- Experiences a lot of negative feelings and fantasies about the receiver

- Feels that she or he must behave in an artificial or restricted way around the receiver

Perceptions About the Message

Because of all of the factors mentioned above, the messenger believes that his or her message will be highly threatening to the receiver. This may be a message that:

- Negatively labels the receiver's character

- Raises concerns about the receiver's ethics, integrity, or morality

- Suggests a decline in the receiver's credibility or reputation

- Suggests a significant level of incompetence or an unacceptable standard of performance

- Offers negative views or information about individuals very close to the receiver

- Directly challenges the receiver's authority or self-interest

Alternatively, the message may involve subject matter that makes the messenger highly uncomfortable, often raising subjects that the messenger sees as:

- Highly personal, such as religious beliefs, sexuality, or politics

- Inappropriate to the work environment

- Requiring the use of certain terms or language that the messenger finds offensive

If, as you read through these lists, you find characteristics that match your situation, then you are facing a tough case. The most important, unifying theme within tough cases is the messenger's strong negative view of the receiver, particularly of the receiver's intentions or motives.

Other Factors

Hidden within these perceptions held by the messenger can be other factors that contribute to making the situation particularly complex. They might include:

- The power the receiver possesses over the messenger, either formally (such as a supervisor's power over an employee) or informally (such as an employee's ability to resist formal authority)

- Larger social issues or long-standing patterns of interpersonal mistrust between the messenger and receiver, including strong negative labels that may exist on both sides, such as "racist," "dictator," or "back-stabber"

- High stakes, such as the potential for immediate and lasting damage to a relationship; a snap decision that could lead to immediate career damage or a decision to leave the organization; or behavior or decisions that could dramatically affect the business or reputation of the organization

- A strong sense of frustration for the messenger, because none of the communication and relationship-building skills that he or she possesses seem adequate to the situation (including those read about in this book!)

How to Approach a Tough Case

Given the obstacles that can be present, you must ask yourself in a most serious way whether you are willing to risk the probable repercussions in return for the potential benefits to you and your organization. If you decide that you are willing to go ahead, taking a well-thought-through approach can greatly reduce the risk you face. Handling a tough situation relies on the same steps and many of the tips outlined in Part Three. In fact, the overall process is no different. It is still wise for messengers to move through their conversations with the same six sequential steps in mind:

1. Get ready for the conversation.
2. Open the conversation.
3. Present your message and motivation.
4. Talk about your message with your receiver.
5. Wrap up the conversation.
6. Follow through.

The difference is that once you've decided to speak up, tough cases demand much greater attention to two of these steps

159

than less risky and less complex messenger situations. In the two chapters that follow, advice is offered for those two: getting ready for the conversation and talking about your message with your receiver. Another story will illustrate those suggestions; it combines several of the aspects that can make a situation difficult. Concerns about the receiver's personal behavior are at the heart of the situation, with negative impacts being experienced in both work outcomes and working relationships.

Sam's Story: "It Looks Like You're Having an Affair"

Sam was the staff assistant to the director of a large county's department of transportation. At the age of thirty-six, he was considered a fast-tracker in public service and looked forward to increased involvement and advancement as the years moved ahead. In his role, Sam was responsible for legislative policy and external relations with state and local agencies. His boss, Duane, the director, was appointed by the county executive, who was an elected official. Sam had worked for Duane off and on for the last ten years. Duane was a seasoned agency administrator, who played the politics as well as most. He was in his early fifties, tough for some to deal with, and known as a person it was better not to cross. Many people, including Sam, had seen signs of a vindictive streak.

Rumors about Duane's affair with one of the work group secretaries had been rumbling for almost a year. And, in fact, even though Sam did not care to know any of the particulars, Duane was increasingly visible when he stopped by her work space, then left the building with her for what appeared to be a two- and sometimes three-hour lunch. Of course, it didn't help that Duane was married. This kind of public behavior fueled the internal rumors, which in recent weeks had become known outside of Transportation as well. More than once Sam had been asked to "talk to Duane about this." After all, it was widely believed that Duane listened to Sam and even tolerated disagreement from him. When people would tell Sam their concerns, he listened politely, but he managed to avoid responding to any of these requests for several months. This was not the kind of issue Sam was comfortable talking about.

160

In the last two weeks, however, Sam had overheard two county commissioners joking about "Duane's extracurricular activities over there in Transportation." This only compounded the discomfort he felt when the woman's manager approached Sam, asking for advice. She said that she felt she could no longer supervise Duane's friend or ask her to account for her time. Sam knew that he needed to do something. Not only was Duane's credibility seriously at risk, but the image of the organization was being compromised as well. These rumors—regardless of the truth—were also jeopardizing the secretary's reputation and her ability to work successfully with others. "Who knows," Sam thought, "what kind of sexual harassment charges might come out of all this before it's over. That's the last thing this agency needs."

Sam saw good reasons to say something to Duane, but none of those reasons did much to reduce the knot in Sam's stomach. It was true that he and Duane had known each other for a long time. Sam believed that Duane respected him. But there was no way that their communication could ever be classified as personal. Sam hoped that Duane would see that his motivation for speaking up was his concern for the agency, yet he knew that Duane might easily see such action as breaking the code of their relationship and that he might quickly tell Sam to "mind his own damn business." If that happened, Sam had no idea what kind of fallout might hit him. Perhaps saying something about the rumors would be seen as "crossing the line" by Duane. What that might mean for Sam's career in this political system was a big unknown. It had all piled up: the visibility; the high stakes of a political environment; the increasing amount of embarrassing gossip; the personal, sexual nature of the issue; and Duane's capacity for retaliation. All of these things created an enormous and confusing fog of feelings and thoughts for Sam.

Clear on his motivation, Sam began to carefully frame his message. He actually wrote out various ways of telling Duane about the rumors. He spent time imagining how Duane might respond. Although he was not sure, he figured that Duane's first response would be an angry, to-hell-with-them reaction. Sam was not a man who was comfortable with angry confrontation, yet he knew how to be patient and he knew how to listen. He figured that those two qualities would be a big help. Mostly, he hoped that the sincerity of his message and his own integrity would have a positive influence on Duane and help him to listen to what needed to be said.

When they began their meeting, Duane thought that Sam was there to take care of a variety of legislative updates. Sam did cover a couple of lightweight, quick issues. Those completed, he opened up his conversation about the rumors by saying, "Duane, there's something else I need to bring up. It's

161

personal, and something you need to address right away." Duane looked a little confused, as if he didn't know whether Sam was talking about himself or Duane. When he said, "Sure, go ahead," Sam clarified his motivations by saying, "I'm here because I care about you and about this agency and its credibility." Duane looked at Sam hard and replied, in a clipped tone, "Sam, you're making me nervous with all this setup. Get to the point."

With a deep breath, Sam said, "Okay, I will. Here goes. I'm a little nervous myself, so bear with me. There are lots of rumors circulating about you having a relationship with Elizabeth over in Construction Planning. It's reached the point where people are talking and laughing about it publicly. It puts us all in a tough spot, especially you. It's time for you to take some kind of action to counteract what's going on."

"Come on!" was Duane's reply. "What kind of fool do you think I am, anyway?" Sam had seen Duane's flashes of anger before. He waited while Duane paced in front of the windows in his office. When he came back toward his desk, he glared down at Sam and, in a cold voice, demanded to know who, specifically, was "spreading these outrageous stories." Prepared for this, Sam reiterated his reason for bringing up this subject. "Duane, I'm not here to add fuel to this fire. I'm here because whether you like it or not, whether it's true or not, this is what's being talked about. It's gone on too long. It's starting to undermine what we are trying to do here."

Duane pushed harder on Sam. "What makes you think you can come in here and make these kinds of accusations, son? You're taking what some might call a career risk here." Sam did not back down. Speaking carefully, he said, "That may be true, Duane. In fact, I thought of that before I came here. Let me be clear. I'm trying to let you know what's going on around the organization." His voice raised significantly, Duane shot back, "So what? This territory is none of your damn business. And I don't want to talk about it."

Sam reminded himself why he was doing this. He plunged ahead. "Duane, the word about what people *see* you doing and *suspect* you are doing has gotten to the council chambers. The long lunch hours, the flowers on Elizabeth's desk: it looks like you're having an affair, Duane. That's what people assume and that's how it appears to me. Don't you care?" Having named the issue, Sam continued. "I suspect that people in the Exec's office are talking, too. You know how she feels about this kind of stuff. Frankly, boss, I'm worried about *your* career." Letting that sink in, he continued. "I think you need to do some damage control—soon! This whole thing is taking energy away from getting our budget through the commission hearings. I fear that your credibility is on the line, and that means this agency is not far behind."

"Dammit, Sam," Duane pressed on, "why can't a person live his life without everyone sticking their nose into it? I don't like it and I resent your trying to make it your business." This was not going well, Sam thought, so he shifted gears. "Tell me, Duane, do you really think I'm here to try to persecute you? Just what do you think my intentions are?" "I don't know," said Duane, slowing down a little. "You obviously believe all this crap, too." A long pause ensued that Sam declined to fill. He let his silence speak for him. Finally, Duane continued, "Well, I guess you're here because you think I need to shape up." Seeing an opening, Sam said, "Duane, what I want is for you to address these rumors. You keep hollering at me, but that avoids the issue. For what it's worth, I can appreciate how this kind of talk can make you angry—and hurt your feelings."

"Well, thanks for that, at least," said Duane as he slumped into his chair. Sam waited again, for maybe a minute, then continued with genuine curiosity: "Tell me, has anyone else suggested to you that people were starting to talk?" Duane replied with a characteristic "Hell, no. Do you think anybody aside from you would ever talk to me about stuff like this? People are afraid of what I might do." "That keeps you pretty isolated, I bet," replied Sam. Calmer now, Duane began to open up. "Actually, that's part of why I enjoy spending time with Liz. She's not afraid of me and is willing to call my bluff. Sort of like you," he said with a half grin at Sam. Wanting to keep this going, Sam said, "I worry that if you stay angry, you'll get even more isolated. And then you'll miss your chance to turn this around." Concerned that he and Duane might not really be communicating, he asked, "Am I making any sense with all this?"

"Yeah." Duane sighed. "The sense it's making is that I've got some work to do. Here and at home, I guess." He moved over to a chair next to where Sam was sitting. This time it was Duane's turn for a deep breath. In a quiet tone, he said, "Tell me what you've heard. I'm ready to hear it."

From there, the conversation went on for almost two hours. Sam stuck with the facts and carefully avoided language that appeared to pass judgment on Duane. He talked about the impacts that he was seeing and offered thoughts about how this type of rumor might damage key relationships with others in government. Eventually, Duane asked Sam for advice on what to do to control the rumors. By the end of the conversation, Duane seemed to be grateful for Sam's communication. Duane said that he would immediately meet with each one of the assistant directors to talk about the rumors. Sam left, believing that he had done the right thing. And he knew that although the meeting hadn't been perfect, he had done the best he could. For the first time in a week, he had a good night's sleep.

Within three months, things were different. The rumors were still present, but they had shifted to the back burner. Other, fresher issues were now on the pipeline. Duane paid increasing attention to agency issues and beefed up his visibility among the people in the field. His noticeable energy was welcome to everyone. The two-hour lunches with Elizabeth came to a halt, although Duane confided to Sam that he had filed for divorce. He said nothing to Sam about Elizabeth. Within two years, they were married and both continued working in the agency. When a new county executive was elected, both of them left the organization.

PERSONAL EXERCISES

Story Exercise 17.1. Sam's Challenge

Situation Exercise 17.2. Do You Have a Tough Case?

GET READY FOR A TOUGH CASE

PRIOR TO DELIVERING their sensitive information, messengers faced with tough cases often find themselves focusing on the negative outcomes they imagine might happen once the conversation is under way. If this focus on the situation's negative emotional weight is carried into the conversation, it makes it very difficult to be either effective or successful as a messenger. In a practical sense, the messenger's up-front feelings of fear, anger, or frustration are very valuable. They are saying, "Don't go forward yet. You're not quite ready." To use an image, the messenger is carrying a heavy pack—too heavy to proceed in a useful way—up a rather steep trail.

This chapter is designed to help with the extra preparation that is necessary when facing a tough case. Carrying the backpacking image a bit further, we will help you to unload the pack and reorganize it so that it will be more manageable once you move into your conversation with your receiver.

Getting Ready: The Basic Tips

Chapter Eleven covered advice on how to get ready to speak up about sensitive issues. If you skimmed through that material or have not read it yet, it might be a good idea to look through it now. There, you will find some do's and don'ts that are briefly reprised here. They are:

- Choose a good time and situation in which to deliver your message; do so as soon as possible.

- Set up enough time to be able to fully discuss your message.

- Spend time thinking about and preparing for your conversation.

- Take your receiver's communication style into consideration.

- Be sensitive to how your receiver is likely to react to your message and to other things he or she might be facing at the same time.

- Don't assume that your receiver cannot handle or is not interested in your message.

Each of these points is also relevant to the tough case. The content here is focused on additional suggestions for preparing for the tough conversation, expanding on the third item in the list above. Some of this preparation has to do with what you know or can imagine about your receiver, but mostly, these new suggestions have to do with you and what you are experiencing as a result of your decision to speak up in a tough case.

| TOUGH CASE TIPS | **Getting Ready for the Conversation**

A big part of what makes a tough case tough is not so much the behavior of the receiver, but the messenger's emotional response to the receiver's behavior and potential behavior. If you are facing a tough case, put the pack down for a moment and take a good, long look at what is going on—inside yourself.

Understand the emotions you have about speaking up in this tough case. The decision to speak up in a tough case can trigger strong emotional reactions in messengers as they wonder about what might happen in the conversation with the receiver. These emotions often have a lot to do with a tendency toward worst-case thinking. If you are someone who quickly imagines the worst about an upcoming difficult situation, you may have more vivid reactions to understand. If you are not, your emotions may fall into a calmer, more measured range.

When thinking about the actual conversation, you may repeatedly imagine a worst-case scenario that seems to be inevitable or based on well-established facts. For example, a messenger might say to herself, "I know he'll retaliate. There's not a doubt in my mind. He's done it to others and he'll do it to me." You might find yourself saying these things:

"I'm so intimidated that I'm shaking just thinking about this!"

"I'm just exhausted and at my wit's end!"

"I'm mad as hell that I have to be the messenger here. It's not fair!"

"I don't trust him farther than I could spit!"

In the process of preparing for your conversation, the way to deal with such feelings is to make them conscious and explore how they might influence your actions during the upcoming exchange. Ignoring them does not make them go away. In fact, this often results in the negative emotions' unconsciously influencing communication or other behavior. By mentally experiencing your emotions, by recognizing your potential to act them out in counterproductive ways with your receiver, you can begin to harness the energy they trap. If you are unwilling to look at how you might behave with your receiver, you don't have a very good chance of getting free of these feelings and the negative behavior they can produce.

Sam was reluctant to talk with Duane about the rumors until their serious impact had become more than obvious to him. When he decided to go ahead with his message, he may have thought or said:

> "Why am I the one everyone expects to talk to Duane? Doesn't anyone else around here care enough about what's going on to deliver this news? What about the assistant directors? I'm just his staff assistant!"

> "If he starts hollering at me, I can see myself yelling back. In fact, I can see myself getting so angry because this thing is so stupid and selfish that I'll feel like picking something off his desk and throwing it at him."

> "I can see myself backing off in the middle of the conversation, maybe weakening what I've said at the beginning. I'd do this because of being afraid of how he could ruin me once this thing blows over. If I back off, I'll hate myself for being so weak."

Carefully assess your communication skills and ability to apply recommended strategies. As you begin to work with your feelings about the tough case, conduct a thorough analysis of the communication and relationship-building skills you actually possess. For example, if you feel intimidated by your tough case, think about the skills you are able to use *in the midst of your strong* *emotions,* such as being scared, angry, frustrated, or upset. As a way to help you with this assessment, consider the following list. We have found that even when they are influenced by strong emotions and high risk, it is still possible for messengers to:

- Paraphrase the other person's views

- Pause before speaking

- Speak slowly and distinctly

- Say, "Excuse me, I need a moment to think about that"

- Ask pertinent questions

- Stay focused on the issues rather than getting sidetracked by the receiver

- Ask for feedback

You may also want to go back to the earlier chapters of Part Three. Review the various tips for conducting the conversation. With your emotions squarely before you, check off the tips that you feel confident you can use now, even when your emotions are strongest. Highlight the ones that you really want to be able to use in the future. Then make a plan to practice those skills with a friend, a colleague, or a spouse—anyone who can give you accurate feedback about how well you are doing.

Be sure to also look over the "Basic Communication Skills" section in the Messenger's Tool Box. As consultants, we have often found that people claim to possess these skills—and they do, just not when things get tough. Even if you feel that you are an effective communicator in most situations, take a look at the skills through the screen of the question: "How do I behave under stress?" You may find that you need to integrate some pieces into your repertoire a little further.

As Sam prepared for his conversation, he imagined how his talk with Duane might go. He was confident of his ability to be patient and to be a good listener. During the conversation, he was patient. He paused several times and did not allow himself to be rushed into saying things that he did not want to say. He also sincerely said things to draw Duane out. One way he did this was by acknowledging that he understood the effect that learning about the rumors had on Duane. In spite of the difficult message, this was a way of connecting to Duane in a human way, and it opened the door to discussing what needed to be done.

Rehearse the way you will express your message, your motivation, or other things you might say if your receiver becomes emotional or resistive. There are two ways to practice what you will say and how you will say it. Both are based upon what you *anticipate* might happen in the conversation. They cannot prepare you completely, because you can never fully predict what you or your receiver will do in any given moment of a conversation. However, this type of practice can help significantly.

One way to rehearse is with a trusted friend or colleague. You will get the best results by actually role-playing the conversation. Try it several ways, having your friend play the part of the messenger while you play your receiver. Then change roles, with you as the messenger. Or you can talk to yourself. Do it when you won't be self-conscious. Play the scenario several ways, adjusting your words and the tone of your voice to convey the meaning and feeling that you want to have in your conversation. Write out a detailed script, challenging yourself to identify the tone of voice that you would use. Then say your lines to see if they sound real to you.

This type of rehearsal may feel awkward and silly, but it can help a lot. In tough conversations, you probably will never use the exact words you create in your rehearsal, but you will go into the conversation more relaxed and confident of your "lines." You will be clearer about the points you want to make and how to make them. As emphasized in Part Three, the more relaxed you can be, the easier it will be for your receiver to relax as well. This feeling will go a long way toward making your conversation a true dialogue rather than a tension-filled confrontation. Sam took the time to write out various ways of expressing his message to Duane and tried to imagine how Duane would respond to what he said. Anticipating that Duane's first reaction would be an angry one, Sam had a clue as to what he needed to be ready to say when the conversation actually took place.

Use affirmations to help you approach your conversation with a constructive and confident attitude. An affirmation is a positive and true statement about yourself that will help you to behave the way you want to in a difficult situation. Athletes use them. People losing weight use them. Messengers in tough cases can use them too! At the end of Chapter Four, we mentioned the phrases or guidelines that have helped us in our work, and in our personal lives as well. We repeat them here:

> "I'm here to build a collaborative relationship, not to be right."

> "I'm here to identify and solve a problem, not to place blame."

> "I can influence the outcome of this conversation, but I cannot control it."

> "I am willing to do the hard work necessary to create understanding."

> "I will share all relevant information with integrity."

> "I am clear about what I am trying to accomplish."

> "I trust myself to be okay, regardless of how this turns out."

Affirmations are very personal mottoes that say something about your philosophy of life. They are a quick reminder about who you are and how you want to behave. It is easy to use affirmations. Once you identify a handful of them (you don't want to have too many because it is hard to remember them), write them down on two or three slips of paper, or on note cards that are easy to flip through. Carry them with you in your car, purse, briefcase, or jacket pocket or on your clipboard.

Prior to your speaking-up conversation, review your affirmations and, as you think about each one, picture yourself living out that particular affirmation. In your mind's eye, see yourself living up to that positive statement about yourself. In particular, use your affirmations to imagine how you will handle tough moments in the conversation. Think of a moment in your imaginary conversation when it would be easy to get defensive and then, remembering the affirmation, imagine how you could turn the moment around or let it go without reaction.

Affirmations that Sam might have written and reviewed include:

> "Duane and others respect me for my honesty and my views, even if they don't agree with them."
>
> "I am a good listener in tense situations."
>
> "I've been in difficult situations before and done fine."
>
> "If all this falls apart and I need another job, I have good connections in the community."

Focus on acceptance. *Acceptance* is your willingness to work with certain realities or characteristics of the people and dynamics involved in your speaking-up conversation. Once that work is completed, it is your willingness to emotionally let go of the remaining elements that you cannot influence or change. You can explore these three aspects:

1. Acceptance of the tough situation in which you find yourself willing to speak up

2. Acceptance of yourself as a messenger

3. Acceptance of your receiver

As an important aspect of preparing for a tough-case conversation, review the questions in Grid 18.1. They will help to highlight your level of acceptance.

It was clear that Sam accepted his situation. When he overheard the comments made by the county commissioners, he knew that something had to be said to Duane. He accepted the fact that he should do it, even though there was a risk and even though he was uncomfortable with this type of subject. Sam also accepted Duane, all his bluster, and his past record of getting back at people. He stuck with his purpose and did not allow Duane to get him off the subject or force him to back down. He

Acceptance of . . .	*Key Questions to Consider*
The situation: When you decide to speak up, you place yourself within a set of complex circumstances.	Are you willing to deal with the negative consequences that might result from your bringing your message forward? Why or why not? Can you move ahead with positive energy, even though the situation may not be fair, fun, or how you had intended to spend your time? Why or why not?
Yourself as a messenger: You bring both strengths and flaws as a messenger that may surface during and after the conversation.	After carefully preparing to deliver and talk about your message and motivation, will you be okay with yourself if your receiver does not understand your point or take the action you want? Why or why not? If negative consequences happen to you or others after your conversation with your receiver, will you be okay with yourself for having tried your best? Why or why not? If you do not conduct yourself in the way that you had hoped during your conversation, will you be able to learn from your experience and let it go? Why or why not?
Your receiver: Like you, your receiver is a person with strengths and flaws that may surface during and after your conversation.	Are you willing to set aside negative judgments or assumptions about your receiver so that you can better understand his or her world as it relates to your message? Why or why not? Are you open to truly listening to what your receiver has to say about your message, even if he or she disagrees with your point and does not want to take action? Why or why not?

Grid 18.1. Acceptance: Key Questions to Consider.

kept presenting the message, never judging Duane but simply focusing on the issues and need for action. Sam also revealed his acceptance of himself when he was able to acknowledge his nervousness to begin with and when he asked whether he was making any sense.

If you find yourself low on acceptance, rethink your decision to speak up. As a result of answering these questions about acceptance, you may find that you are overly worried about experiencing negative consequences. You may also realize that you have a hard time imagining yourself being "okay" if you try your best and do not succeed. If either of these situations is true for you, then you may want to rethink your decision to speak up. Go back to Part Two and rethink the points and Personal Exercises connected to Chapters Eight through Ten.

It is far better to reevaluate the decision to speak up at this point than to go ahead into a complex situation where you are not ready to accept yourself if things do not go well. The bottom line is this: *If you don't trust yourself to be okay if it goes badly, then don't go ahead.* If that is the case, Chapter Ten will help with strategies for increasing your readiness to speak up or finding other ways to get your message through.

 PERSONAL EXERCISES

Situation Exercise 18.1. Talking Out Your Emotions

Situation Exercise 18.2. Your Skills Inventory

Situation Exercise 18.3. Creating a Script for Your Conversation

Situation Exercise 18.4. Your Affirmations for a Tough Case

Situation Exercise 18.5. Your Level of Acceptance

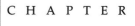

19

TALK WITH YOUR RECEIVER IN A TOUGH CASE

DECISION TO SPEAK up—reconfirmed. Backpack—reorganized and ready to go. What's left, of course, is your conversation with your receiver. In this chapter, we want to provide some helpful techniques that build on the preparation tips that were called out in the last chapter. Our purpose here is to increase your sense of safety and self-confidence as you talk to your receiver about your message in a high-risk situation.

The do's and don'ts we recommend for handling a tough case meld interpersonal communication skills with acceptance of yourself and your receiver. The interaction with your receiver should be a dialogue, an exchange of views between two people that results in increased understanding. This can happen even in tough cases. The key, however, is being able to stay true to your purpose and being able to accept—rather than judge—the flaws that both you and your receiver bring to the situation. When the methods of communication we suggest here and in Chapter Fourteen are applied in the framework of that acceptance, both you and your receiver will have an easier time engaging in a conversation that leads to mutual understanding and support for the action you desire.

Sam's story will continue to illustrate many of our suggestions. Since "words to help me get started" are particularly valuable in tough cases, additional examples will be provided to give you a greater understanding of how some of these tips can be applied.

Talking About Your Message: The Basic Tips

As in the previous chapter, we'd like to begin by reminding you of the nine suggestions we offered for talking with your receiver about your message in normal speaking-up situations. You might want to review them more carefully by turning to Chapter Fourteen. Briefly, they are:

- Listen carefully to the receiver's perspective about your message, especially if she or he seems to resist what you are saying or becomes emotional.

- If you can, offer additional information to help the receiver understand the importance of the issues to you.

▪ Don't make negative assumptions about your receiver's or others' intentions.

▪ Use neutral words to describe the behavior or circumstances that are creating problems, not phrases that communicate blame.

▪ Stay open-minded to what your receiver says; don't discount the receiver's reaction to your message or jump to conclusions based on your own biases.

▪ If you find yourself getting emotional, describe your feelings rather than acting them out.

▪ Look for opportunities to ask for feedback about your message or your manner of bringing it forward.

▪ If it is appropriate, discuss what you are willing to do or what you have already been doing to deal with the situation.

▪ If possible, offer ideas about what to do next.

| TOUGH CASE TIPS | **Talking About Your Message with Your Receiver** |

The additional suggestions made for tough cases are designed to address the increased emotion and tension that may be present in these very difficult situations. In particular, they pick up on ways to more fully listen, address negative assumptions, and build in a safety net for you if you find that your emotions are too strong for you to continue.

Remember your purpose. Tense and complex conversations may drift in many ways, whether by sliding off into less threatening subjects or by verging on personal attacks. When things get off target, your job as a messenger is to bring the conversation back to your message. In Sam's conversation with Duane, he voiced his purpose at least three times. Notice how in the third comment, he smoothly avoided getting sidetracked by Duane's demand to know who was spreading rumors.

"I'm here because I care about you and about this agency and its credibility."

"It puts us all in a tough spot, especially you. It's time for you to take some kind of action to counteract what's going on."

"I'm not here to add fuel to this fire. I'm here because whether you like it or not, whether it's true or not, this is what's being talked about."

Here are some other examples that you might find helpful:

"Sung, I think we are off track here. I'd like us to stay with the discussion of the argument we had last week. I brought this up so that we could improve our working relationship. That's the reason I came to talk with you today."

"Turell, I can only say again that I believe our company is suffering from a lack of leadership. It's a perception that I think involves you. I wouldn't be here if I didn't believe that this could be worked out."

Make observations about the dynamics of what you see happening. One of the most helpful interventions in emotional situations is simply to report on what you see happening. The observations serve as a brief check on how things are going, rather than on the content of what is being said. This enables both parties to work on changing the tone of an exchange in order to get it back on track. To make such observations, it helps if you use neutral words to describe both the verbal and nonverbal dynamics of the conversation. Sam did this by saying, "You keep hollering at me, but that avoids the issue."

Here are more examples you might find helpful:

"I can see that this is uncomfortable for both of us. We seem to be pushing one another's buttons. This conversation is a lot angrier than I thought it would be."

"Julien, you are frowning and pacing. I don't know what that means."

"When we started talking, it seemed like things were going to go well, but now we seem to have gotten all tangled up in a lot of bad feelings. Maybe we need to talk about that."

Share your feelings. Perhaps the most immediate and powerful thing a person can do in a tough exchange is to describe the emotions that she or he is experiencing at that moment. In a way, this is similar to observing the dynamics in the conversation, except that the focus is on how the person speaking is feeling in the moment. Sharing your feelings can enable you and the receiver to go to a deeper level of connection and understanding in the conversation. Sam acknowledged both his feelings and those he observed in Duane when he said, "I worry that if you stay angry, you'll get even more isolated."

Here are some other expressions of feelings:

"I feel discouraged. I thought we had agreed to some rules of the road in how we would communicate. We don't seem to be doing such a great job."

"I'm really happy that we've had this conversation. It went so much better than I had imagined!"

"Help me through this. Every time you mention your commitment to the project, I start getting frustrated because I wonder how real that commitment is."

Listen completely to the other person without judgment. It is tough in a difficult exchange to allow someone else to speak without interruption. Your brain cells fire constantly with evaluations of what the other person is saying. The tougher the exchange, the more difficult it is to set aside your internal reactions and fully listen to the other person. Great patience is required. Discipline yourself to stop the judgment process and listen all the way through, getting the other person's full story before moving on.

Do this by paraphrasing and asking questions that probe and clarify the receiver's thoughts, feelings, or experience.

Sam demonstrated this mostly by listening to Duane as he reacted. Sam didn't allow himself to be bullied by Duane, nor did he get pulled into defending himself against Duane's accusations or threats. At one point, he asked an important question that triggered some revealing comments from Duane. Sam said, "Tell me, has anyone else suggested to you that people were starting to talk?" Shortly thereafter, he paraphrased Duane, which encouraged Duane to talk at an even more heartfelt level. Sam said: "That keeps you pretty isolated, I bet."

Here are other examples:

> "It sounds like you're saying that I don't have all the facts and have no right to speak with you about the promotion process in your division. Tell me more about this. I want to try to understand your point of view here."

> "This is an awkward silence and I guess I could barge in with my own thoughts. But I get the sense that you feel that I can't appreciate your views. Give me a chance with that. Tell me what you really think."

> "Lattice, when you talk about "the fear of failure" in the project, I feel like it's the tip of an iceberg. If you're willing, can you tell me more of your side of things?"

Share your negative assumptions. In Chapter Fourteen and elsewhere, we advised you to avoid making negative assumptions about your receiver's or others' intentions. This is hard to do, especially when mistrust is present. However, in tough cases it is even more likely that you will have negative assumptions about your receiver's intentions, and you may need to talk about them directly. This is exactly what may make your situation a tough case. If you cannot set these negative assumptions aside, they may be a core part of your message.

In a situation like this, pull the negative assumption out onto the surface and label it for what it is, *an assumption*. Describe the behaviors or events that have led to this assumption. Sam worked hard to avoid making negative assumptions about Duane's intentions, but he worried about Duane's vindictive streak. When this began to interfere with Sam's presenting the message about the rumors, he chose to put the issue on the table by stating out loud his assumption that Duane was having an affair. He also named specific behaviors that had led to these conclusions.

Here are other examples:

"José, I have to tell you that you've come across to me as somewhat evasive. That may not be your style or your intention. I may be wrong about this opinion of you, but when I try to discuss our work together, you do tend to change the subject. You're doing it right now and I believe that it's hurting our chance to talk. Do you feel that you need to avoid an open discussion with me?"

"Esther, I can't help but feel that sometimes you behave in manipulative ways. Here's what I've seen you do that's led me in this direction. You've selected people for positions without discussing the matter with me, even though we agreed that this needed to happen. You made a budget request directly to the board. You've been in my office discussing others negatively, as if they were incompetent and I should take action against them. I consider these things quite serious. They make it look as if you're trying to control things behind the scenes rather than through open communication of your ideas and opinions."

"Sid, I'm sorry to have to say this, but you appear to me—and to others—as insensitive when you're handling tough situations at the front counter. I recognize that the word *insensitive* is a label, but here's what I've seen that causes people to use this word: raising your voice, not answering the phone, and not helping when someone else asks for help. If I don't share this with you, I don't know how this self-managing work-team concept is ever going to get off the ground."

181

Ask for feedback about the negative assumptions your receiver may have about you. This is a particularly important strategy if you are trying to overcome mistrust through the messenger process. It is helpful when negative assumptions are involved and you have surfaced some of your own. Allow the tables to be turned. At one point, after he had sincerely expressed his motivation several times, Sam asked Duane for this kind of feedback. He said, with a bit of exasperation, "Tell me, Duane, do you really think I'm here to try to persecute you? Just what do you think my intentions are?" With the assertive application of this tip, Sam pushed Duane into reevaluating some of what he had been saying. It was at this point that Duane began to be more thoughtful and less bombastic in his comments.

Here are other ways to do this:

> "I've shared my opinions, Felice, and I know I covered some sensitive ground. Maybe you could give me an idea of how my own behaviors may have gotten in *your* way."

> "This has been a tough exchange and I worry that I'm communicating too strongly. Tell me, am I coming across too abrasively? Am I sounding like a jerk?"

Reschedule or extend the discussion. Sometimes, even with the best of intentions and skills, people get stuck. They get stuck because they don't know what to do or say next. They get stuck because they are too emotional—or emotionally too exhausted—to go further. If a conversation becomes too intense, you always have the option of closing it off in favor of a later time. This time-out may be ten minutes or two days. The point is that this break allows sufficient time for you and the receiver to get your bearings and try again. This was not necessary for Sam, but here's how others might handle this situation:

> "I'm very uncomfortable and don't feel like I can continue this conversation right now. Can we talk again at four o'clock? I need some time to cool off and rethink my message."

"I'd like to extend this discussion. We have other points to discuss and we are both out of time. When can we come back to this?"

"I need a break. Let me get a cup of coffee and come back. I'm pretty churned up and don't want to leave things like they are right now."

Engage a third party. A useful strategy when the conversation is anticipated to be—or becomes—too complex or too tense is to bring in a third person who can serve in a neutral capacity to help your conversation reach a positive conclusion. Third parties typically play one of three roles:

1. As a *facilitator* to ensure clear, safe communication between you and your receiver

2. As an *expert* who has certain necessary information or insight that neither you nor your receiver possess

3. As an *authority figure,* usually someone at a higher level in the organization, who can bring a larger perspective to your discussion or resolve a conflict between you and your receiver by making a decision and enforcing it

If you are anticipating a tough exchange and would like this support, discuss it with your receiver in advance. Or, as in the previous suggestion, if you get into the conversation and then discover that a third party would be helpful, bring up this idea. If your receiver agrees, collaborate on selecting someone to be of assistance. As quickly as possible, arrange a time when the three of you can meet. Here are some examples of approaches:

"Xiang, I want to talk with you about how the materials transfer process is going between our departments. After the exchange we had last Thursday, I thought that we needed someone who has more information. Together, you and I are simply pooling our ignorance and getting nowhere. I thought that Tom could give us some help. What do you think?"

"I want to stop this conversation until we can get someone to help us. I think we're stuck. Can we agree on someone to facilitate this discussion?"

"Pete, I'd like to suggest that we ask Lonnie to help us sort this thing through. We disagree—that's obvious. And we can't reach an agreement that we both can support. Since he's in charge of this project and we aren't, maybe he'll have some information that could help. Or maybe he'll be the one to decide. Is that okay with you?"

It is important to note that in some conversations, especially those between co-workers, a messenger may raise issues that have to do with the receiver's poor, uncooperative, or damaging performance. If, through the speaking-up steps outlined in this book, the receiver refuses to change, the messenger may need to go to a higher authority in the organization, even if the receiver does not agree. Some situations can't be handled by the messenger alone. When the organization's mission is at risk or liability or ethical issues are in the balance, a smart and courageous thing to do is to seek the support of someone with greater organizational authority.

 PERSONAL EXERCISES

Situation Exercise 19.1. Improving Your Script

Situation Exercise 19.2. Discussing Your Negative Assumptions

Situation Exercise 19.3. Asking for Your Receiver's Assumptions

PART V

SUSTAINING THE COURAGE

LEARNING TO FLY

The messengers you have met through the stories in this book demonstrated a willingness to face difficult and risk-filled situations. They prepared for, delivered, and discussed some very sensitive issues that are a part of everyday work life. Most of them were successful. A few were not. Take a moment to review their names and their situations.

- Sarah, who as a manager persisted in her efforts to get her peers, her president, and her vice president to take constructive action on the breakdown of communication and leadership in her division

- Shawna, an administrative assistant, who decided to pass along her observations about the leading candidate for a job who she felt was not qualified

- Bernice, a young assistant head nurse, who asked her administrator for help during a staff shortage

- Chris, a member of a staff unit in a manufacturing plant, who took his friend and boss, Jamal, to lunch to say that in Jamal's absence the work group was falling apart

- Ted, working in a plant shipping department, who spoke up to a co-worker who was not doing her fair share of the work

- Terri, an internal consultant, who discussed with her boss her fears about a possible reduction of the scope of her job and her worries about being treated unfairly by him

- Tyrone, who, as a member of a team getting ready to select a vendor of premanufactured parts, informed his boss, Don, that Don's favorite bidder on the contract was not qualified

- Angela, the director of organizational effectiveness who informed her new boss of the policy against drinking alcoholic beverages at work-related social functions

- James, who first individually, then in a group meeting, told his executive vice president that the planned market expansion was the wrong product and with the wrong partner

- Betsy, who confronted her co-worker, Lois, about Lois's use of racial slurs

- Adam, the young sales representative who spoke to his managers about wanting their coaching so that he could improve his skills in the field

- Benito, the social worker who had to determine why his colleague, Pam, did not follow through on her commitment to deliver nutritional information to the mother of an under-weight infant

- Sam, a rising star in a county governmental agency, who finally gave feedback to the agency's director about credibility problems related to rumors of the director's affair with a secretary

Does their experience end after their conversations are over? What, if anything, comes next? Sustaining the courage is the final phase of the messenger's experience. Sustaining the courage is

about continuously maintaining and building upon the spirit that enables a messenger to deliver and discuss the tough news. A chapter covers each of the following steps:

1. Slowing down to reflect on and learn from each speaking-up experience

2. Speaking up repeatedly, each time getting better by building on the learnings from previous experiences

3. Using the skills and success developed over time to positively influence the organization and help it to become receptive to those who bring forward tough issues for discussion

Getting Better at Bringing Forward the Tough News

To sustain their courage, messengers must commit to improving their ability to talk about difficult subjects. As with any other skill, getting better at speaking up takes concentration and persever-ance. The payoff can be a big one, for the messengers and for their organizations. There are three compelling reasons to make these improvements:

1. *Doing so enhances personal integrity and self-worth.* When people do what they believe is the right thing in the face of risk, it reaffirms the strength of the personal values that guide their lives. They can see how their messages lead to positive change and they recognize that they have played a small part in strengthening their organizations.

2. *Doing so reduces frustration and increases pleasure in the work environment.* On a practical level, frustrations can disappear or be reduced. Time and money can be saved. Tensions in relationships can be eased. All of these set the stage for increased energy, creativity, accomplishment, and fun.

3. *Doing so contributes to the strength and health of the organization.* A free flow of information, insight, and ideas within an organization increases the likelihood of ongoing organizational success. Quality products and services can be delivered more quickly, new ideas spark improvements and innovations that delight customers, and waste and rework are reduced, resulting in a lowered cost of doing business. This type of success, in turn, increases the chances of longer-term health for the business.

As you read the next three chapters, you will find an underlying challenge presented to you. This challenge will ask you to consider yourself in the future and to ask whether or not you can see yourself playing a more active messenger role. If you can, and if you want to become a more skilled and more successful messenger, study the next three chapters; they will assist you along that part of the messenger's journey.

HOW DID IT GO? WHAT DID YOU LEARN?

THE CYCLE OF SPEAK-
ing up, first presented
in Figure 1.1, begins
when a person recognizes the presence of
a problem or opportunity that would
make things better in some way if it could
be discussed. It continues through the act
of delivering and discussing the message
and concludes with reflections and learning from the experience. This last phase,
the evaluation of the messenger's experience, is the topic of this chapter.

Four Questions for Reflection and Learning

To accelerate and enhance the learning process, a messenger should slow down to consciously review the speaking-up conversation. The following questions should then be carefully considered:

1. Did I do the right thing?

2. Did I do it well?

3. Was it well received?

4. Did it make a positive difference?

On the surface, these questions might appear to be logical prompts to a simple yes-or-no response. If you slow down, however, they can lead to a set of in-depth and thought-provoking observations and conclusions. As you reflect on each of the questions:

■ Be honest in your evaluation of how things went.

■ Concentrate as much on the aspects of your conversation that went well as on the things that did not.

■ Give yourself credit for trying to make a positive difference by taking the risk to speak up. Additionally, give yourself a pat on the back for taking the time to reflect on your experience so that the next time you speak up you are better prepared to do so.

■ Explore the circumstances behind your initial answers. Consider the reasons why things happened the way they did. This will give greater depth to your reflection and enable you to learn more from your experience.

Did I Do the Right Thing?

This question is about your original decision to speak up, not about how well you did. It asks you to evaluate, in an overall way, whether your decision was a sound one. Your answer will reflect the personal values and beliefs that guide your general sense of right and wrong. These additional questions may help you to arrive at your answer:

- If I had this to do over again, would I speak up? Why or why not?

- Am I proud of the fact that I raised this issue at this time? Why or why not?

Remembering that "hindsight is always 20-20," it is useful to reflect on the soundness of your decision to speak up in light of *what you knew or believed at the time you made your decision.* Based on what you knew then, not what you know now, was it the right thing to do? If the results of speaking up have revealed serious errors on your part in interpreting the situation, you should ask yourself, "What happened? How did such a misjudgment take place?" In these instances you will need to evaluate your decision in light of what you know now, in order to determine whether or not you truly did the right thing.

Did I Do It Well?

This question should cause you to think about your personal expectations of your performance when talking with your receiver. It asks you to stand outside yourself and compare how you *wanted* to deliver your message with how you *actually* talked and behaved. As you think this through, be careful to separate how you did from how your receiver responded. You may have done everything you could to ensure a successful conversation, yet other reasons, well outside of your influence, caused your receiver to react negatively.

Was It Well Received?

Sometimes you will see clear indicators of a receiver's reactions. In other circumstances, you may have to hunt for clues as to how the message was received. It is important to keep in mind that a negative reaction during the conversation is not the same thing as not receiving the message well. While hearing your message, your receiver may have had strong emotional reactions that you interpreted as negative. Yet by the end of the conversation, you and your message might have been very well received. To more accurately assess your reception, think about what your receiver said—both verbally and nonverbally—to indicate that he or she:

- Understood your message and motivation or agreed to take action to address your concerns

- Disagreed with your message and would not take action on your behalf

- Was suspicious of your motivation for bringing your message forward

As with the question "Did I do it well?" remember that even though you may have been at your best—focused, clear, open, and appropriate—your receiver still may have had a negative reaction to your message, motivation, or request for action.

Did It Make a Positive Difference?

This question focuses on the results of your conversation. To determine these outcomes, you might want to return to the reasons why you decided to speak up in the first place. Do the outcomes in any way match the benefits you hoped to see as a result of sharing your concerns or ideas? Phrased another way, this question could be: "When all is said and done, was it worth all I went through to bring my message forward? If so, why?"

Keep in mind that the positive difference we are talking about might not be exactly what you asked for or imagined. Consider the following chain of unanticipated benefits:

■ Perhaps you asked for a pay raise, but as part of the discussion, you realized that the real source of your frustration was how your job was defined. If you and your receiver sorted this out and made good decisions, you may have left the conversation feeling that a positive difference had been made, even though your pay did not go up.

■ Another surprise might have come if, at the end of the discussion, you gained some insight that deepened your respect for your receiver.

■ As a result of taking the risk to speak up, you may now see that you can express your interests and desires without repercussions and with more poise than you previously imagined to be possible.

Unexpected results such as these are clear rewards for slowing down and taking the time to reflect and learn. Without doing this, the unanticipated positive results may never be revealed.

Situation Exercise 20.4 contains additional questions that are designed to illuminate, in more detail, your experience when answering the four questions. Grid TB 5 in the Messenger's Tool Box can be used for recording your answers.

Guidelines for Learning

Here are some general reminders that may be useful after you answer the four questions for reflection and learning.

IF YOUR ANSWERS ARE "YES" OR MOSTLY "YES"

1. You might want to ask yourself or others, "How is the receiver of my message doing?" Even though your answers to the questions are mostly "Yes," your tough news may have hit your receiver particularly

hard. Following up to see how she or he is doing may be a way to strengthen a new or existing relationship.

2. Things may have gone exceedingly well for you and your receiver. If so, express your appreciation for this mutual good work. Such comments will help to solidify your positive working relationship.

3. Consider what your success says about how you are developing as a skillful and successful messenger. You might want to compare this experience to ones you have had in the past to gain some sense of your own improvement.

IF YOUR ANSWERS ARE MOSTLY "MAYBE" OR "NO"

1. Avoid being harsh or perfectionistic. Remember that as only one person in a conversation, you cannot control the situation. You can only do your best to clearly express yourself and constructively influence your receiver toward a positive outcome.

2. If you end up with a lot of "Maybe" or "I'm not sure" answers, don't be put off by the ambiguity or uncertainty you discover. Push further to understand the reasons for these responses.

3. When you identify things that you truly could have done better, translate these mistakes into ideas that you might use to your advantage in the future. Once you understand the factors that contributed to the problems, let go of any lingering frustration, embarrassment, or guilt. Hanging on to these feelings will only make it harder for you to take a similar risk in the future.

What Happens Next?

Answering the four questions may identify some important next steps that need to be taken. Consider the following possibilities.

Follow-up work should be done related to your recent conversation. This can fall into two categories. The first is *repair work.* It might include additional conversations with your receiver that are intended to:

- Receive or share feedback about your recent conversation

- Apologize, if this is appropriate

- Talk about perceptions of repercussions

- Redo the first conversation more effectively

Finding the courage to go back for the second conversation may be as tough as speaking up in the first place. If things did not go well, you may feel the tug of cynicism or increased fear pulling you backward. Your willingness to initiate additional conversations defines your level of commitment to the message and to your relationship with the receiver. If you did not read Part Two too closely before, it may become helpful now.

You also may want to *reinforce the positive outcomes* of your conversation. To do so, you might:

- Do whatever you said you'd do, then report back to the receiver about the results

- Through these same methods, find out what your receiver has done to act on the commitments you made together

195

You discover an indication of a right or wrong "fit" with the receiver, your job, or your organization. Although it is not likely, it is possible that your speaking-up conversation represents a pivotal moment in your current job, your relationship with your receiver, or even your career. Such a dramatic moment is certainly not what people normally think of as an *everyday* act of courage. But it can happen, from both a positive and a negative perspective. If it does, you may find that your messenger experience has illuminated:

- A delightful recognition that you are in exactly the right place at the right time

- An unacceptable disparity between your own values and the realities of your organization

Much more common is an *indication* of a fit, whether it is comfortable or distressing. This less intense experience is important to take note of, especially if it points in the direction of a mismatch of values. If the experience is negative, recognize that your insight may eventually lead you to make a conscious choice about continuing to stay in your organization.

You realize that you would like to continue to speak up in the future. If you believe that speaking up is the right thing to do and that you have the potential to be increasingly successful as a messenger, then you may want to:

- Pay particular attention to the motivation that inspired you to speak up in your most recent conversation

- Anticipate other situations that might come up where the same motivation might again cause you to say something

- Think of other reasons that could cause you to set aside your worries about the risk that might be present

You want to know how you might do things differently in the future. If you recognize a need and a desire to improve so that you can be more effective the next time you decide to speak up, you may want to:

■ Replay your memories of your preparation and the conversation with your messenger

■ Think about how you could have done things differently and achieved greater success

■ Consider going back to your receiver and asking for feedback on how you might have presented your message, your motivation, or yourself more effectively

You discover a desire to significantly improve your ongoing ability to bring forward and discuss tough issues. Whether your recent speaking-up experience was positive or negative, you may sense that the role of messenger appeals to a core personal value. If so, you may decide that you truly want to become a more skilled and successful messenger. A decision of this kind requires a commitment of time and spirit, because reaching a high level of skill and success does not happen overnight. This decision is the conscious departure point for a unique journey into unexplored, exciting, and demanding personal territory. It is a journey of personal transformation.

 PERSONAL EXERCISES

Situation Exercise 20.1. Should You Evaluate Your Speaking-Up Experiences?

General Exercise 20.2. Your Reasons for Wanting to Improve

Situation Exercise 20.3. Answer the Four Questions

Situation Exercise 20.4. Thinking About "Maybes" and "No's"

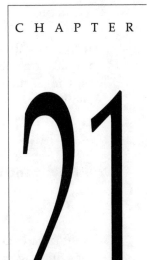

THE MESSENGER'S TRANSFORMATION

I F YOU COMMIT TO becoming a highly skilled and successful messenger, you will also become a different person through having made that choice. The change may seem subtle at first. But over time, it will become more obvious and have a powerful impact. At one point, you will probably look back and recognize that prior to your commitment, your thoughts, feelings, and actions about workplace communication were based on a different framework. As you reflect on your former self, you will understand that you have turned a significant corner in the road.

The Personal Transformation

Messengers who have experienced such a turning point often have the feeling that they never want to go back or, more profoundly, that they are "not able to be the same again." This type of change can be called a *personal transformation*. By this, we mean that a person is different in a significant way because some important belief or value has changed or an important insight has occurred. This shift then becomes a new principle for action that causes noticeable changes in a person's behavior, feelings, and thoughts. These two elements—the recognition of a deeply felt personal shift and a change in behavior that is based upon that shift—are the primary components of personal transformation.

When a person begins to speak up more frequently, it is a sign that some fundamental shift has taken place. Consider the possibilities presented in Grid 21.1. Shifts such as these are often not noticeable until long after they have occurred. That is why many experienced messengers will look back on a period of time and recognize, after the fact, that a change has taken place and they have become significantly different as a result of their willingness to speak up in a repeated fashion.

Sarah Eastland's Transformation

In Chapter Two, we told you about Sarah Eastland, a messenger who found the courage to speak up to her peers and those above her in the hierarchy. As a result of her conversation with her vice president, Dave Trimbull, an organi-

Beliefs in the Past	Current Beliefs
Others are not interested in what I have to say.	I have a point of view others find valuable.
It's not my job to identify problems.	I have a responsibility to raise concerns about things that make work more difficult.
If I say what I think, I will get in trouble.	If I clearly say what I think and tell people why it's important to me, they will listen.
If I get in trouble for speaking up, my chances for success will be over.	If I get in trouble for speaking up, it will help me to learn how to more effectively convey my message in the future.
I shouldn't speak up all the time because others will think I'm a know-it-all.	I have a responsibility to raise issues, concerns, and questions.
I may say the wrong thing or hurt someone's feelings.	I am able to say hard things so that others can hear the point without taking it personally.
I can't criticize upper management—it is too risky.	I have ideas and information that are helpful to the success of those in leadership.
People who speak up are just trying to rock the boat.	People who speak up are demonstrating their commitment to the organization.

Grid 21.1. Past Beliefs and Current Beliefs.

zational upheaval was avoided. This happened because Sarah, Dave, and many others worked hard at overcoming their previous counterproductive patterns of behavior. Sarah's willingness to take the risk of coming forward triggered a series of events that made a significant and positive impact on the company. But what about Sarah? What happened to her?

Eight years later, Sarah is still with the same company. She eventually left her managerial position in order to pursue other interests and now serves in a unique function. "Right now," she says, "even though it's not my job title, my role is as an internal change consultant. I hear a lot from operations people about senior management. And I hear a lot from senior executives about operations. I help them come together. To bridge the gaps. All the time."

When he is asked about Sarah's contribution over time to the organization, Dave remembers that eight years ago "she helped us all to see that we needed to deal with the core issue of how we work together as a team. Even though we didn't know it at the time, that's how she helped to prepare our division for our efforts to improve quality. In this way she also helped the rest of the company to move ahead. Over time, she's retained and lived that core value." Dave describes what he and his colleagues at the executive level are doing. He says, "We are trying to create a lean organization, by flattening things and getting the bureaucracy out of the way so people can do their jobs. In this effort, we need constant clarity about what we are doing. Sarah helps to create that clarity by raising issues, making observations, and keeping us focused."

Dave also has experienced the personal impact of Sarah's growth as a skillful, courageous messenger. "As a corporate leader, I don't have to constantly worry about missing something important. She will either coach others to speak up or she'll speak up herself. That way, I hear about the things I need to know. And when she does speak up, it's powerful. She's more respected than ever because of her personal integrity."

Further describing what she does at work, Sarah comments, "I get the undiscussables on the table. If you don't get these issues out, the other stuff can't happen. Subterranean issues will cause tunnels, which will cause the ground to collapse."

Reflecting on her speaking-up experiences of eight years ago, Sarah acknowledges the risks she took, the fears she faced, and the way she has changed. "Now I'll do anything by myself. I have no qualms about saying the things that need to be said—in the moment. Sometimes I wonder if I have pushed too far. I worry that I appear cocky to others. But I have developed the confidence to deal with the situation. I can get a bead on something and it is usually right on." With a little probing about how she is able to be so skilled and have a relatively easy time putting tough issues in front of people for discussion, she adds, "I know the company. I also don't have any personal agendas in these situations. I never divulge what people tell me in confidence—and I know that they know that. All this helps. Plus, over the years, I get more and more experienced."

How Personal Transformation Happens

Sarah's development as a skillful and courageous messenger symbolizes much of what the final three chapters of this book are all about. Over the last eight years, she has gotten better and better at bringing the tough news forward. She recognizes this, as do others. In fact, her ability has been so appreciated that her current job has been structured so that her understanding of the messenger role and her personal messenger skills can be fully utilized. The experiences she has had, the effects she's seen, and the acknowledgment she has received have combined, shaping a personal transformation. She admits that things haven't always gone easily, but she sees those moments as an important part of her continued improvement as an effective messenger. She has been conscientious about reflecting on her experiences, especially the ones that didn't go so well. She has also stuck with the messenger's journey.

People like Sarah become highly successful messengers by *repeatedly* bringing tough news forward. The more times that a person senses a need to speak up in a risky situation, finds the courage to overcome the risk involved, decides to speak up, delivers and talks about the tough issues, and reflects on and learns from the experience, the more quickly he or she will develop the level of skill and confidence that is so much a part of Sarah Eastland's experience. Repetition of these steps builds the experience that will cause the messenger to look back and say such things as:

"I guess I *am* different now."

"I could never go back to the way I used to handle these situations."

"I recognize that situations that used to scare me are now relatively easy."

This is the moment when personal transformation is recognized. When you are in this situation, you might not be able to fully describe the shifts that have taken place under the surface, yet you will recognize the impact of those changes by the way your behavior has changed over time. For example, Sarah tells us that she has recognized that she used to be willing to bring a message forward only once. If she received no response, she would drop it. Now the motto that guides her is: "I have a responsibility to raise issues and to work constructively until they are heard."

Steps Along the Messenger's Journey to Transformation

The experience of personal transformation can be a slow accumulation of everyday acts of courage. When that process becomes a conscious one, the messenger's transformation can expand and accelerate. This is shown in Figure 21.1. As messengers set off on the journey to personal transformation, they typically go through the phases described in Grid 21.2. Notice that in addition to a description of each phase, this grid includes suggestions for what you might do when you find yourself passing through any of the phases.

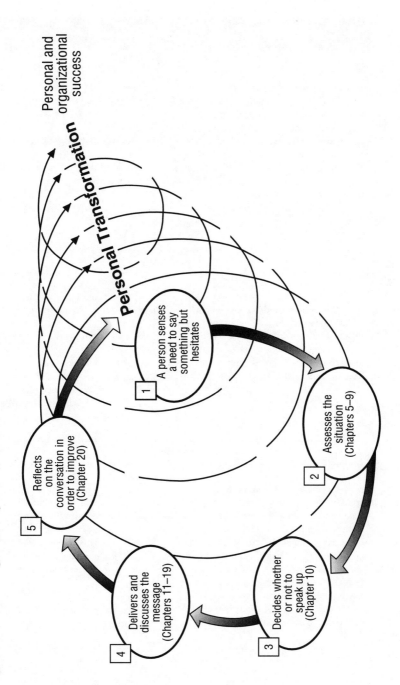

Figure 21.1. The Messenger's Journey of Transformation.

Transformation Phase	*Suggested Action Steps*
Personal Reinforcement	
Messengers experience some type of improvement, however small, which frequently represents a contribution to the organization. At the same time, they recognize a sense of personal integrity that comes from acting according to personal beliefs about "the right thing to do." Both of these can lead to a sense of personal satisfaction and reinforcement, especially when they happen at the same time. This, in turn, can inspire a desire to get better at bringing tough news forward.	Concentrate on two of the four questions we outlined in the last chapter: • Did I do the right thing? • Did it make a positive difference?
Repetition	
Messengers continue to speak up, building on past experience and insights. In particular, mistakes and misjudgments are a powerful source of new learnings. During this phase, messengers often feel awkward. They leave conversations believing that they could have done a better job.	Become rigorous about the remaining two questions: • Did I do it well? • Was it well received? They can trigger important reflections, leading to improved strategies.
Increasing Confidence	
Messengers receive positive reactions about speaking up. This does not happen all the time, but frequently enough to be noticeable. Such recognition from others may be subtle or indirect: a nonverbal pat on the back, appreciative eye contact, or after-the-fact references. This quiet or occasional recognition combines with the personal satisfaction of having made a contribution or done the right thing, reinforcing a positive self-evaluation. Slowly, confidence grows.	Follow up on the subtle reactions of others. Ask someone what was meant by an appreciative look or an indirect compliment. This can be a way to gather more specific feedback about the impact you are really having. Develop personal goals for improvement.

Grid 21.2. Transformation Phases and Action Steps.

Transformation Phase	Suggested Action Steps
Going Deeper	
Messengers continue to speak up, facing increasingly difficult situations. A typical experience for someone at this point is to think back on a recent conversation with a receiver and say, "How about that? A year ago, I never could have said what I just did!" As with any skill, what was once challenging becomes easier. What once required great concentration is now more relaxed and graceful.	Take none of this success for granted. Stay alert to the process of preparation, presentation, and discussion of increasingly difficult messages. Deliberately identify scary speaking-up situations and take them on as a way to continue your development.
New Identity	
Finally, messengers experience a sense of a new identity. At the end of the transformation loop, messengers are clearly able to bring forward and discuss difficult issues. They do so comfortably and confidently. Additionally, many shift their expectations of themselves. They believe that speaking up about the tough issues is something that they *should* do as a part of who they are at work.	Be the person you have become. You may find yourself: • Taking on a self-initiated role as "the person who will say something" when others will not • Moving into a mentoring or facilitative role with others • Sharing what you have learned • Being a positive and engaging role model for others This teaching or coaching action will expand your capacity many times over.

Grid 21.2. Transformation Phases and Action Steps, cont'd.

When Bad News Becomes Good News

Messengers and their receivers *can* survive a tough message. In fact, as with Sarah and Dave's organization, the bad news may become the catalyst for good news down the road.

Sarah is quick to admit that the changes she's made are not always simple or easy. "There are times when I've wondered if it's been worth it. Others have helped me to see the great personal satisfaction I get from my work." She acknowledges "a tremendous sense of accomplishment. I know I've made a positive difference. With all the change we are now experiencing in the business environment, people are again in pain. I want to help us get through it. I want the company to succeed."

Dave's assessment of Sarah's value is to the point: "We want more people like Sarah working here. Lots more. We are focusing our hiring efforts on bringing in more people at all levels with skills and courage like Sarah's. We are trying to figure out how to identify or grow these skills and abilities from within the company as well."

The ability to deliver and discuss tough issues in risky situations is one of the most important interpersonal skills that any of us can develop. The future will increasingly demand this ability of all of us. And, in many organizations, the future has already begun. More and more, organizations recognize the importance of having people like Sarah in all types of positions. People like Sarah, people like you, are making extraordinary contributions to their work environment.

 PERSONAL EXERCISES

General Exercise 21.1. Your Past and Current Beliefs

Story Exercise 21.2. Sarah's Transformation

General Exercise 21.3. Where Are You in the Transformation Process?

CHANGING THE ORGANIZATION BY SPEAKING UP

OUR VISION OF THE future workplace is of a place where people would not understand the purpose of this book and where much of the language we have used here would seem outdated and old-fashioned. The terms *messenger* or *speak up* would seldom be used because people would talk easily about the issues that were important—including the unpleasant ones. People would not worry about their messages or motivations being misinterpreted because everyone involved would be committed to fully exploring anything that might improve organizational performance. The thought that someone would "shoot the messenger" for bringing up a piece of tough news would be as unexpected then as it would be today to find an office without a computer.

A Practical Vision

Depending on where you work, this vision may seem quite practical and close at hand or completely impossible to imagine. Increasingly, organizations consciously build work environments in which disagreements surface easily and complex and messy issues are aired openly. Courage is *not* required in all organizations. As one of our colleagues put it, "In my organization, it's not 'Should I tell,' but 'How *soon* can I tell.'" In organizations such as hers, a critical mass of leaders and employees understands three things:

1. What an organization does not know about itself strongly influences its future success.

2. An unmistakable key to that knowledge is the intelligence that surfaces when tough issues are raised frequently.

3. The most satisfying and productive workplace relationships are those that are characterized by trust, collaboration, and integrity and those where people are encouraged to speak up about their concerns and good ideas.

The Skilled and Successful Messenger as a Catalyst for Change

Skilled and successful messengers have an extraordinary opportunity to be catalysts for positive change in their organizations. By their actions and continued commitment to helping the news to get through, they:

- Encourage others who are less confident to be courageous and to develop speaking-up skills

- Demonstrate the practical value of discussing tough issues to those who might be hesitant or skeptical of the benefits of doing so

Skilled and successful messengers help to build a critical mass of people who understand and act upon the three points mentioned above. Essentially, they use their personal transformation to help transform their organizations. If you want to help your organization to become more open to discussing hard, risky issues, consider the following suggestions.

Work hard to become both skilled and successful as a messenger in your organization. By repeating the cycle of speaking up and paying attention to your experiences, you will continue to improve your skills. The more skilled you are, the more times you will be successful. Watch others who are effective messengers to see what they do and how you might incorporate some of their successful techniques. Use the content and exercises in this book to reinforce your learnings. Reflect on the concepts of courage, risk, and contribution in order to better understand what they have come to mean in your own life.

Serve as a role model for others. Because of your increasing credibility and success, it is likely that others will come to you for advice about how to speak up. Or they may ask you to relay a message for them. Take advantage of these opportunities to become a coach for others. Be a sounding board for those who are

211

trying to sort out the risks involved with conveying a certain message. When they decide to go ahead, help them to identify words and approaches that will increase their chance of success. Be available afterward to help them to reflect on what happened and on useful learnings.

Be a role model for others by exemplifying in your daily routines the affirmations we referenced in Chapters Four and Eighteen. When you conduct your work life around such principles, you will automatically reflect a commitment to honest collaboration and encourage others to do the same.

Encourage and support those who are receptive to hearing difficult messages. Let those who are supportive of messengers know how much you appreciate their efforts. Your recognition of their behavior will reinforce their commitment to build an open, collaborative workplace. These individuals might be excellent compatriots with whom you can strategize ways to encourage others to speak up about and be open to tough news.

Exert your positive influence with a few key people who seem resistant to tough news or unable to hear it. Even in organizations where people are encouraged to speak up, a few individuals may still resist hearing tough messages. Their impact can be quite negative, especially when they are in key leadership positions. Using your credibility and your well-developed messenger skills, help these people to see the value of being receptive to difficult news. You may find yourself delivering personal feedback to them about aspects of their communication style that they have never heard before. The message to deliver is threefold:

1. This organization needs to get as much information as it can about problems and opportunities; that may mean discussing difficult or unpleasant issues.

2. Your apparent unwillingness to hear this type of information is a barrier to our collective improvement; consciously or unconsciously, you seem to be doing things to keep people from saying what they think needs to be said.

3. By being open to listening to and discussing tough news, you will help yourself and this organization to be successful.

Taking actions such as these can make a significant difference. People who do deliver such feedback play a pivotal role in transforming an organization. They help their organization to move from following a set of fear-based, hierarchical beliefs to being oriented around learning and improvement. Some of these shifts are captured in Grid 22.1, on page 216. When a lot of people behave in this way, amazing things begin to happen.

Speaking Up: The Chain of Impacts

Figure 22.1 describes observable trends that happen when large groups of people in an organization either speak up or do not speak up. This model illustrates the way in which an individual's decision to speak up is central to future organizational success. It emphasizes the importance of both your choice to continue to speak up and your choice to influence those around you to do the same.

The chain of impacts points in two directions. One is toward organizational success that is characterized by increased competitiveness and organizational effectiveness. The other is toward staying the same or moving into decline. In both directions, a self-reinforcing cycle of organizational dynamics is created, with one thing leading to another. As you examine the flow in each direction, remember these things:

- It would be unlikely for an organization to ever fully represent only one direction of the model.

- This model focuses on what we see as a desirable trend that should be encouraged and an undesirable trend that should be avoided.

- Every person can play a part to move toward increased collaboration and competitiveness.

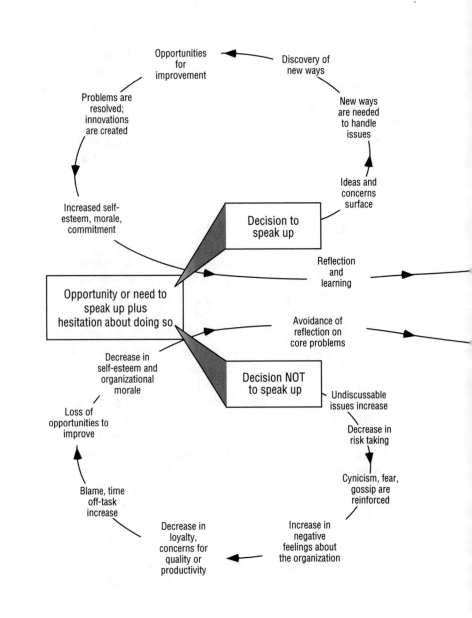

Figure 22.1. Speaking Up: The Chain of Impacts.

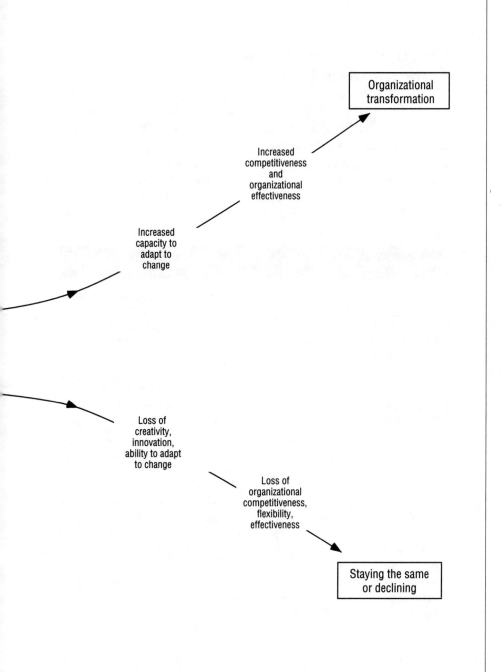

Figure 22.1. Speaking Up: The Chain of Impacts, cont'd.

Moving Toward Decline: Opportunities Lost

Organizations on the downward spiral are often characterized by a reluctance to be open to new ideas, criticism, or alternative approaches. Mistrust is common between work groups, layers of the organization, and key players at all levels. Organizations such as these tend to operate on many of the fear-based beliefs we identified in Grid 22.1. When a significant number of people decide *not* to speak up about their

Fear-Based Beliefs	Improvement-Oriented Beliefs
Information is a source of power and should be shared very carefully as a means of enhancing one's own power base or career.	Information is a source of power and should be shared freely so that everyone involved can use it to improve.
Mistakes are a source of embarrassment and should be punished or ignored.	Mistakes are a source of learning and should be discussed openly.
People who identify problems are troublemakers.	People who raise concerns are a vital resource in the effort to improve.
Loyalty means going along with what the boss wants, regardless.	Loyalty means offering your best skills and critical thinking to help the organization fulfill its mission.
A team player does not question policy or the party line.	A team player participates fully in an open give-and-take of ideas and divergent thinking.

Grid 22.1. Transformation from Fear to Improvement.

concerns or good ideas, the chain of impacts shown in Figure 22.1 can be set in motion.

When repeated, this leads to an eventual erosion of most effective problem solving, productivity, creativity, and innovation. Over time, more and more people become caught in this closed, negative cycle. It becomes increasingly difficult for those who are not afraid or cynical to retain their energy and creativity. The continued loss of information to organizational leaders affects their ability to do anything but react, sometimes too late, to changes in their markets. All this results in a loss of advantage for the organization in terms of flexibility, competitiveness, and organizational effectiveness.

Moving Toward Success: Opportunities Gained

In other organizations, where the critical mass chooses to offer new ideas and surface problems directly, the opposite effect occurs. People feel supported and commit their talents to improvement rather than cover-ups. Creativity, rather than cynicism, is used to adapt to a rapidly changing future. Everyday acts of courage accumulate into a workplace of greater openness and trust. Ongoing relationships are seen as the foundation for solving problems, rather than a barrier to their solution. When a significant number of people decide to speak up, the positive results shown in Figure 22.1 emerge.

Over time, as this cycle repeats itself, the organization will significantly increase its capacity to initiate and adapt to change. More and more, people at all levels will act based on beliefs that are oriented around improvement and learning. When a critical mass of people makes this shift, the organizational culture will have been transformed. In this state, the organization is well on its way toward greater effectiveness, with an increased ability to compete and be flexible in an ever-changing business environment.

Imagine What It Might Be Like if Everyone Spoke Up

Our vision of the future workplace—where words like *messenger* and *repercussions* would be strangely out of place—depends upon a critical mass of people who easily and frequently bring up their concerns and good ideas. Many organizations are well on their way to achieving such a vision. In these environments:

- Building trust and collaboration is part of the strategic plan.

- Leaders understand the power of the chain of impacts—in both directions.

- The talent of each employee is tapped to create excellent decisions, wise utilization of resources, and a level of service that builds a strong and loyal base of paying customers.

- Respecting and utilizing people's intelligence is considered the right and smart thing to do because it builds a foundation of capable people who are committed to success.

- Conservation of time and energy comes from reducing nonproductive activity like hallway conversations that consist of griping, complaining, and speculation.

- Generation of energy and quality comes from people feeling free to work together in different groupings to create ideas, develop plans, solve problems, and evaluate progress.

- "We-they" thinking disappears and criticisms are voiced in the form "*We* ought to do so-and-so" instead of "I don't know why *they* don't do what I think they should!"

- People in all positions are able to focus on the work to be done, rather than on fear, suspicion, or cynicism.

- Collaboration builds a bridge between employees and management so that people say, "We are all a part of this organization."

- People leave work and realize that they have actually had fun.

Imagining such an organization is easier than creating it. To achieve such a vision, many people need to be involved.

Getting the News Through:
Creating Organizations That Are
Not Afraid to Change

Individuals in all positions and their organizational leaders share the responsibility for making sure that the news gets through. It is like a handshake—two people need to participate fully for it to be satisfying and in order for it to work. An individual messenger, no matter how skilled or successful he or she is, cannot transform an organization. Neither can leaders, no matter how gifted, enlightened, or committed they are. Everyone in an organization must do his or her part to help the enterprise move successfully into the future.

In the best of situations, leaders do their part to make the organizational changes that allow messengers to find a receptive audience for their concerns and ideas. And, in the best of situations, individuals do not wait for a risk-free environment before they speak up. Courage is required on both sides.

Yet the rewards are great. One reward, which comes when many people easily and frequently bring forward their concerns and good ideas, is the promise of improvement. Improvement in the work that gets done, in the environment where it takes place, and in the relationships at the center of each person's work experience. These improvements make it possible for an organization to face a turbulent future with hope and enthusiasm.

The president of one organization that broadly encourages speaking up puts it this way: "First of all, I am choosing this strategy on purpose. I see the benefit of it every time I attend one of those CEO forums. People ask me, 'Why aren't you in the middle of gloom and doom?' It is because our primary effort is in developing the ability to handle change. The secondary issue is handling a specific change itself. All these other folks are talking about implementation and tactics. They are not talking about mind-set or capacity." Appreciating the advantage he and the others he works with are experiencing, he adds, "Here, we aren't as frightened as many because we acknowledge that we don't know what is going to happen. But we are clearly developing the ability to handle whatever comes along."

Mind-set and the capacity for change. That's what everyday acts of courage are all about. More and more every day, people share both creative and critical thinking—along with information and insight. The mind-set says, "I'm concerned about what we are doing. I've got an idea that might help." The capacity for change encourages others to listen openly and try a new approach.

With many people involved, building over time, courageous messengers create enormous capacity within their organizations. In such organizations, *risk* is a concept that applies to the marketplace rather than to communication in a staff meeting. *Courage* guides the future vision of the organization, rather than what individuals need to get through the day. And people throughout the organization work together to create a workplace community where mutual success, credibility, and integrity truly flourish.

 PERSONAL EXERCISES

General Exercise 22.1. Four Suggestions for Action

General Exercise 22.2. The Chain of Impacts

General Exercise 22.3. The "Critical Mass"

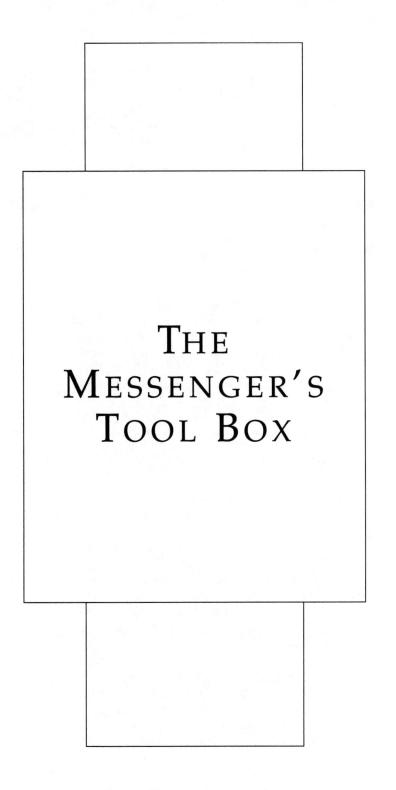

THE MESSENGER'S TOOL BOX

PERSONAL EXERCISES

How to Use the Exercises

The exercises in this section can serve as a resource as you read the main text and work to apply the principles of speaking up. Presented by chapter, they focus on the most important learning points and themes found in the book. The exercises are designed to be used in the following three ways:

1. As a catalyst for deeper mental reflection

2. As a means of sorting through specific situations

3. As a comprehensive journal of your development as a courageous messenger

A Catalyst for Mental Reflection. As you read each chapter, these exercises pose questions that can help you to integrate key points into your own thinking. To increase your learning, evaluate how the exercises connect directly with experiences in your work life and your desire for improvement.

A Means of Sorting Through Specific Situations. Some of the exercises will help you to evaluate real scenarios that you are currently facing or could face in the future. This work can help you to see how to incorporate important principles into your personal messenger challenges. Select the exercises that will be most important to you and use extra sheets of paper to write out your responses to them. Sample grids or other formats are frequently suggested to support your learning process.

As you work through the exercises, you can also use the ten-point Speaking-Up Summary Sheet to help prepare for specific conversations. These pages consolidate the points you will want to remember as you speak up and later evaluate your experience. Several of the exercises (referenced on the Summary Sheet itself) can help you in working with this useful guide.

A Comprehensive Journal.   You may wish to work through all the exercises—some of them once, others several times—as your skills increase. If you choose this option, consider making your own journal notebook with many blank pages to record your work. This journal could become a long-term companion as you follow the spiral of the messenger's journey. It could include responses to exercise questions, messenger summary sheets, and a diary of experiences, questions, learnings, and successes. This journal could be a living record of your improvement path as a messenger.

TYPES OF EXERCISES

The exercises are divided into three types:

1. *General exercises:* Use these to push your thinking about chapter themes and major learning points.

2. *Story exercises:* Use these to gain insight into the dynamics of the messenger stories presented.

3. *Situation exercises:* Employ these when preparing for your own speaking-up challenges.

Speaking-Up Summary Sheet

Create your own Summary Sheet using the format below and complete through item 9 before speaking up. Complete item 10 after speaking up.

Receiver _____ Date _____

1. **My true message:** *(Situation Exercise 6.1)*

   Situation:

   Impacts:

   Possible causes:

   My request:

2. **My real motivation:** *(Situation Exercise 7.1)*

3. **The probable risks:** *(Situation Exercise 8.1)*

4. **Contingency plans:** *(Situation Exercise 8.4)*

5. **My yes-buts:** *(Situation Exercise 9.1)*

6. Some affirmations I want to remember: *(General Exercise 4.2 and Situation Exercise 18.4)*

7. Phrases to help open the conversation: *(Situation Exercise 12.3)*

8. Phrases to foster specific agreements: *(Situation Exercise 15.3)*

9. Other tips and pointers I want to remember:

10. Evaluation: *(Situation Exercise 20.3)*

   Did I do the right thing?

   Did I do it well?

   Was it well received?

   Did it make a positive difference?

   Are there any negative repercussions?

Follow-up steps

   Learnings for the future: what I will try to do better next time

The Exercises

CHAPTER ONE: WELCOME TO THIS BOOK

General Exercise 1.1. Your Reasons for Reading This Book. Think about your learning objectives for reading *The Courageous Messenger.* Which of the following categories is most nearly like you?

> "I do not really know how to speak up at work very well and want to learn to do so."
>
> "I know how to speak up but am reluctant to do so as often as I would like."
>
> "I already speak up but would like to increase my skill and grace as a messenger."

Based on your answer, identify several wishes or hopes about what this book could bring you.

General Exercise 1.2. Responsibilities of Leaders and Messengers. This chapter makes the point that leaders alone cannot create safe work environments, free of blame and repercussions. They must also depend on their partners, courageous messengers, in this effort. Create a pie chart that shows what part of the responsibility you believe belongs to the leaders and what part belongs to messengers. Then make a list of what you believe are the specific responsibilities each has for creating a safe, open environment.

CHAPTER TWO: COURAGEOUS MESSENGERS

General Exercise 2.1. Your Experience with the Three R's. Review the descriptions of the Three R's in the main text. Then respond to the following questions about each of them.

Imagine a working *relationship* in which speaking up about tough subjects involved no courage at all. Have you personally experienced working relationships like this? In your own words, how would you describe what they are like?

What *risks* and *repercussions* related to speaking up have you personally experienced in the past? What beliefs about speaking up do you now carry with you as a result of these experiences?

What *rewards* for speaking up have you personally experienced? How have these experiences shaped your desire to be a skilled and courageous messenger?

CHAPTER THREE: MESSENGERS AND TOUGH NEWS

Story Exercise 3.1. Challenges Faced by Shawna, Bernice, and Chris. This chapter presents three stories about courageous messengers. Analyze each story in light of the Three R's presented in Chapter Two.

What is the *relationship* between the messenger and the receiver and how do you think it has been affected by the messenger's speaking up? Does it become stronger and clearer or has it been damaged? Why?

What *risks* does the messenger face? How realistic do you believe these fears are? What does each messenger do to prepare to take the risk of speaking up?

What *rewards* does each messenger hope for? Why do you think each messenger decided to proceed in spite of the risks?

What do your answers to these questions say about the way messengers make a decision to speak up? How does this relate to you and your own experiences as a messenger?

General Exercise 3.2. What Type of Messages Do *You* Send? Take a look at Figure 3.1, "What Messages Are About." Consider several situations of your own in which you felt a need to speak up but experienced some hesitation in doing so. For each situation, describe the content of your message in terms of work outcomes, working relationships, and personal behavior.

Not every situation might involve all of these characteristics. Where more than one overlapping circle is involved, identify the circle that was most important to you as the messenger and the one most important to your receiver. If they are not the same, what implications do you see for how you might have approached speaking up?

CHAPTER FOUR: BECOMING A SKILLED MESSENGER

General Exercise 4.1. Your Observations About Skilled Messengers. This chapter offers key principles about skilled messengers. Based on what you have read, begin to develop your own vision of what it means to be a skilled messenger. Start by defining for yourself the difference between *skilled* and *successful*. What do these two words mean to you?

Now, think about situations where you have observed others speak up—colleagues, a member of your family, a friend. What did you notice about the messenger's approach? What did the messenger do especially well? What could have been different? Did you see this person do anything that reflects the principles outlined in Chapter Four? If so, which ones? What other principles, based on your own experiences, would you add to the ones listed?

General Exercise 4.2. Your Own Affirmations. Consider the seven affirmation phrases at the end of the chapter. Which one or two in the list are most important to you as a messenger? Why? Are there others, not listed, that are as important or more important to you personally? Write these out in a concise way so that they are easy to remember.

General Exercise 4.3. Restating Affirmations as Behaviors. Based on your answers to Exercise 4.2, try to restate two or three of your key affirmations as sets of specific behaviors you want to exhibit as a messenger. Ask yourself, "What do these affirmations really mean to me in terms of action and conduct?" Put your key affirmations on the left-hand side of a sheet of paper and put behaviors on the right-hand side. See Grid TB 1 for an example.

CHAPTER FIVE: COURAGE IS AN INSIDE JOB

General Exercise 5.1. Reflections on Courage. Spend a few moments with the word *courage*. What does this word mean to you? When have you seen other people show courage? When have you shown courage personally? Where do you believe more courage is required—in taking the initial risk or in facing the consequences? Why? What does your answer tell you about your own challenges as a courageous messenger?

Story Exercise 5.2. Terri's Challenge. What are your reactions to Terri's story? What moment in her speaking-up story would you point to as the most courageous on her part? Why?

What do you think gave Terri the courage to speak up? Do you see her as a naturally self-confident person? What role do you think her values played in her decision to be a messenger?

Situation Exercise 5.3. Your Speaking-Up Case Study. Identify a specific speaking-up situation that you would like to use as you work through the rest of the book. To get the greatest benefit, the situation should be something you are facing now, not a past situation you want to evaluate. Who is the receiver? Briefly, what is the situation about?

CHAPTER SIX: KNOW YOUR TRUE MESSAGE

Situation Exercise 6.1. Your True Message. Follow the steps outlined in the text to find your true message. Use Terri's extensive example as a guide for doing this work.

Situation Exercise 6.2. Did the Process Work for You? Once you have completed the analysis in Situation Exercise 6.1, assess its value to you. By slowing down to consider each of the points, did you discover anything new about the situation, its impacts, its causes, or possible receiver actions? Which step was the easiest for you to do?

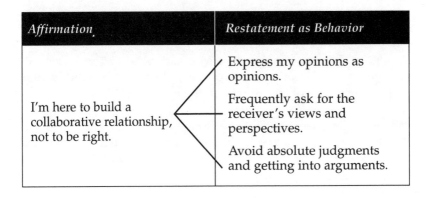

Affirmation	*Restatement as Behavior*
I'm here to build a collaborative relationship, not to be right.	Express my opinions as opinions.
	Frequently ask for the receiver's views and perspectives.
	Avoid absolute judgments and getting into arguments.

Grid TB 1. Affirmations and Behaviors.

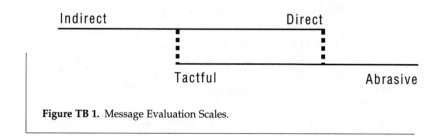

Figure TB 1. Message Evaluation Scales.

Which was the hardest or least comfortable? Why? Do you feel more confident about your message now? Why or why not?

Situation Exercise 6.3. Testing for a Direct, Tactful Message. True messages are honest, clear, direct, tactful, nondefensive, and focused on the core of the messenger's concerns. They are neither indirectly nor abrasively worded. Indirect and abrasive statements are on opposite ends of two important scales, shown in Figure TB 1. An indirect statement obscures the true message with excessive tact or watered-down phrases that end up confusing or frustrating the receiver. An abrasive statement comes across as blaming, judgmental, and demeaning, or as sarcastic or threatening.

Look back at the message statement you have drafted. Where would you place it on these two scales? Does it fall on the overlapping section of the two scales or over to one side? Are you satisfied with its placement or should you redraft the language?

CHAPTER SEVEN: KNOW YOUR REAL MOTIVATION

Situation Exercise 7.1. Your Real Motivation. Use Terri's example as a guide to completing the steps for finding your real motivation. Create the grids or tables shown in the text if you like.

Situation Exercise 7.2. Did the Process Work for You? Do you feel that you were successful in identifying your real motivations? Did this exercise help you to gather additional courage to step forward? Why or why not?

General Exercise 7.3. Hurtful Messages. Identify some possible examples of messages based on overly self-focused or hurtful motivations—for instance, suggesting a "work improvement" that intentionally shifts the burden to others who are already overloaded or using the goal of speaking up as an excuse to put down someone else in a damaging interpersonal conflict.

What might cause a person to get hooked on self-focused messages and motivations in the first place? What should a person do who finds his or her motives mixed with negative, hurtful factors? Can you see the potential for more positive messages and motivations hidden in the two situations listed above?

CHAPTER EIGHT: ASSESS YOUR RISK

Situation Exercise 8.1. Your Risk Factors. Review the list of risk factors in Chapter Eight. Which of these factors would apply to your speaking-up situation? Do you know of other factors, not listed, that would add to the probability of repercussions?

Situation Exercise 8.2. Assess Your Risk. Once again, follow the steps outlined in the text to assess the level of risk in your situation. Use Terri's example as a guide for your work, creating the scales shown in the chapter.

General Exercise 8.3. Instances of Worst-Case Thinking. Create your own examples of worst-case thinking about small events or facts that have been blown out of proportion, either by you or by others. Think back to times when you or someone you know "catastrophized" about something that might happen but never came to pass. What was the stimulating event? What conclusions or possibilities were inferred? What type of logic drove the worst-case thinking? What specific emotion?

Situation Exercise 8.4. Your Contingency Plans. If you have decided to go forward, develop a set of responses or contingency plans for the repercussions that you are concerned might occur. This could include planning what to say or do if the repercussion occurs during your meeting with the receiver and if it occurs later.

As you review these contingency plans, also consider their impact on others, such as members of your work group, employees, supervisors, and family members. Do you need to bring them into the loop before speaking up?

Situation Exercise 8.5. Did the Process Work for You? How effective was Chapter Eight in helping you make the risks of your situation more visible? Do you feel more or less comfortable proceeding as a result? Why?

CHAPTER NINE: UNDERSTAND YOUR YES-BUTS

Situation Exercise 9.1. Your Yes-Buts. Continue your analysis according to the framework laid out in the chapter. Use the grids and other formats displayed for Terri's example.

Situation Exercise 9.2. Did the Process Work for You? Did Chapter Nine help you to surface other, unexpected impediments to speaking up? What has been the long-term impact of these patterns on your life at work? How can learning to speak up more effectively influence these patterns?

CHAPTER TEN: MAKE A DECISION

Situation Exercise 10.1. How You Feel About Your Decision. As you select one of the five options, identify your emotional reactions to it. For example, are you elated, eager, calm? What is causing you to feel this way? If your feelings are mixed, write them down, showing how they may be balancing or counteracting one another. For example, you may be *tense* about following through, but *glad* and *relieved* that you have decided to go for it. Or you may be *uncertain* about delaying a decision to speak up, but *comfortable* that it is a prudent thing to do. Is this mixture of emotions a cue to revisit the options? Or are you ready to go on?

Situation Exercise 10.2. Your Decision-Making Style. Do you tend to make decisions quickly or to defer them? Notice how your natural decision-making style is influencing your choice of options. Do you need to modify your natural style or put it on hold in order to make the right decision? How would you go about stretching your comfort zone in this way?

CHAPTER ELEVEN: GET READY FOR THE CONVERSATION

Story Exercise 11.1. Tyrone's Challenge. What makes Tyrone's situation one in which preparation is crucial? Since Tyrone obviously has an ongoing relationship with Don, why wouldn't he just lay out his concerns in an informal, off-the-cuff way? Do you believe that would have been a better approach? Why or why not?

Situation Exercise 11.2. How You Want to Communicate. Imagine the key words, phrases, sentences, and thoughts you want to communicate during your conversation above and beyond your core message. Write them out on a sheet of paper and critique them. Consider whether they are honest, direct, nondefensive, clear, and tactful.

Review and rewrite these words until you are comfortable with them, then review with a friend or colleague. What advice does your associate have? Try to arrange the phrases and sentences in the order in which they are likely to come up during the conversation. Use this as the outline of a script for the conversation. Are there some blanks you need to fill in?

Situation Exercise 11.3. Your Receiver's Communication Style. Thinking about the last few conversations you have had with your receiver, describe his or her communication style and approach. Identify patterns in the way your receiver prefers to talk through issues. Then decide how this might influence your approach as a messenger. Use the approach displayed in Grid TB 2.

CHAPTER TWELVE: OPEN THE CONVERSATION

Story Exercise 12.1. Angela's Challenge. Angela made the assumption that Phillip had no knowledge of the company's alcohol policy. Suppose it had been clear that Phillip knew what the policy was and consciously decided to violate it. Would that have altered the way Angela approached him and opened the conversation? In what ways? What opening words might she have used in that case?

Story Exercise 12.2. What About Steve? Should someone say something to Steve? Who should do this and what should the message be? What words could be used to open that conversation?

Patterns	Approach
Likes to talk around a subject for some time before committing; won't be pushed into a quick decision	Allow more time than I am personally comfortable with to discuss the issues Be willing to explore the same aspect of the message several times from several different perspectives; be prepared to do so Allow the receiver to have some "soak time"; don't try to force a decision at this meeting
Enjoys humor; uses funny comments to break tension	Avoid being utterly serious; smile; use a tone that balances a serious issue with not taking life too seriously Reflect on some situations we have shared and gone through together, ones we can laugh about now though at the time they were tough

Grid TB 2. Adapting to the Receiver's Communication Style.

Situation Exercise 12.3. Know Your Opening Lines. List at least five different phrases you might use to open the conversation with your receiver. Use the scales in Figure TB 1 in Situation Exercise 6.3 to evaluate each statement. Which do you feel will best reduce tension? Which will be most effective with your receiver? Why?

CHAPTER THIRTEEN:
PRESENT YOUR MESSAGE AND MOTIVATION

Story Exercise 13.1. James's Challenge. Were there elements in James's story that remind you of your situation? If so, what are they? If you have ever "been shot" in public, like James, how did you handle it? If you were in his position, would you have conducted yourself any differently in the meeting?

Story Exercise 13.2. What About Eileen? Should James have a talk with Eileen now that the meeting is over? If so, what might be his message to her and his motivation? What specific words should he say to her?

Situation Exercise 13.3. Your Receiver's Interests. What do you believe the "enlightened self-interest" of your receiver to be? If you have not done so previously, brainstorm benefits to your receiver from acting on your advice. Then list the negative effects of not acting on this advice. Go back and review which statements are still too focused on your own interests. See if these can't be rephrased. Use what you have learned from this effort to shape your presentation of your message and motivations.

Situation Exercise 13.4. Effective Request Statements. Consider the following request parts of two hypothetical messages:

"I'd like you to wipe out the old deadline for the team."

"Would you just stop long enough to hear about this customer's problems?"

Each of these leaves something to be desired in terms of being specific, assertive, tactful, nondefensive, or complete. Do you see any possible negative assumptions leaking into these requests? How could each request be rephrased? Now, write out your own request and subject it to a similar critique.

Situation Exercise 13.5. Say Your Message Out Loud. Practice saying your full message out loud, starting with the situation, its impacts, its potential causes, and your request. Have a colleague listen as you role-play what you want to say. If no one is available to help you, talk into a tape recorder. Listen for parts of your rehearsal that would be confusing to your receiver or cause defensiveness. Practice clarifying what you mean.

CHAPTER FOURTEEN:
TALK ABOUT YOUR MESSAGE WITH YOUR RECEIVER

Story Exercise 14.1. Betsy's Challenge. What would you say is Betsy's interpersonal strategy for dealing with Lois's reactions during their conversation? How would you describe the impact she has on Lois as they talk? What do you believe that Lois most appreciates about Betsy? What do you think that Betsy most appreciates about Lois?

Situation Exercise 14.2. Asking for Feedback from Your Receiver. Identify one or two points in your conversation with your receiver where you might ask for feedback. What phrases would you use to do this? What concerns might you have about using this strategy? What advantages can you see?

Situation Exercise 14.3. Know Your Assumptions. Identify the assumptions that you make about your receiver's intentions, motives, or character. First describe your receiver's behaviors, then what they mean to you. These assumptions may be positive, neutral, or negative. Select the ones that are negative and convert them into more neutral statements, as shown in Grid TB 3.

CHAPTER FIFTEEN: WRAP UP THE CONVERSATION

Story Exercise 15.1. Adam's Challenge. Why do you think Adam did not focus on specific agreements and a follow-up plan with Karen and Peter? What might have held him back?

Story Exercise 15.2. What About Karen and Peter? What negative assumptions, after the fact, would it be easy to make about Karen's and Peter's intentions? What other explanations could account for their behavior?

Receiver's Behaviors	What I Believe These Behaviors Mean About the Receiver's Intentions, Motives, or Character	Neutral Assumptions I Could Make
Uses agendas, takes notes at meetings, likes to clarify objectives	Organized when approaching problems (neutral)	
Keeps door closed most of the time	Thinks he's better than others; wants to shut them out (negative)	He's okay with a high level of privacy and distance from others

Grid TB 3. Behaviors and Assumptions.

Situation Exercise 15.3. Moving the Conversation Toward Agreements. How open do you believe your receiver will be to moving into specific agreements? Will this person feel that you are overcontrolling the situation? What statements could you use to help turn the conversation toward action planning without resistance? Identify a few phrases you believe your receiver will be open to—for example, "It feels to me like we've nailed down the situation and some general thoughts on how things should change. I'd appreciate it if we could come up with some specific agreements on what to do next."

Situation Exercise 15.4. Imagining Your Follow-Up Agreements. Use Grid 15.1 to create an imagined set of positive follow-up steps for your meeting with your receiver. Freely list your hopes for specific action items. Fill in every column, if you can. How might filling out this chart in advance help you to clarify your message and influence the way you choose to express it?

CHAPTER SIXTEEN: FOLLOW THROUGH

Story Exercise 16.1. Benito's Challenge. What emotions did Benito experience when he found out that Cindy had not received the nutritionist's new information through Pam? What things did Benito do to help himself avoid becoming too hooked on his own negative assumptions?

Situation Exercise 16.2. Your Own Follow-Through. What might prevent you from following through on agreements you make with your receiver? Why? What should you do if you feel that you cannot meet them?

Situation Exercise 16.3. Staying Flexible. What are some specific ways in which you will need to stay flexible and open if your receiver does not follow through? How will you combat negative assumptions about the receiver if this happens?

Situation Exercise 16.4. Planning a Second Message. Build on Situation Exercise 16.3 by describing how you might speak up a second time if your receiver does not follow through. Using the steps described in Part Two—know your message, know your real motivation, assess your risk, and understand your yes-buts—quickly outline what it would mean to go back to the receiver for another conversation. Would you decide to speak up a second time? Why or why not? How might this hypothetical evaluation of failure to follow through help you to assess your current situation and decision to speak up?

CHAPTER SEVENTEEN: DO YOU HAVE A TOUGH CASE?

Story Exercise 17.1. Sam's Challenge. From your standpoint, what makes this a tough case? If you had been in Sam's shoes, what would have been the factors foremost in your mind as you considered a possible decision to speak up? Is this a reflection of a barrier that is particularly important to you when handling tough cases?

Situation Exercise 17.2. Do You Have a Tough Case? Go through the lists at the beginning of the chapter (beginning with "Perceptions About the Receiver") and check off the phrases that you feel pertain to your situation.

Get specific about the items you have checked off. Think through (and write down) why you selected each item. What specifically is it about you, the situation, the message, or the receiver that seems to match the criteria listed? To what degree do you feel you *must* communicate negative assumptions about the receiver in order to get your message across? Why?

CHAPTER EIGHTEEN: GET READY FOR A TOUGH CASE

Situation Exercise 18.1. Talking Out Your Emotions. When you are sure you are facing a tough case, it can help to talk through your feelings. With someone you trust, discuss your worst-case scenario in detail, focusing on what could go wrong in terms of your own behavior. Some ways to think about this include asking yourself:

- At what points might you feel especially vulnerable in the conversation? How might you behave in those moments?

- What could happen that would cause you to act with too much emotion?

- What might you say or do that you would not be proud of later?

Situation Exercise 18.2. Your Skills Inventory. As described in the text, conduct a thorough inventory of your communication skills *under stress.* List the skills that will be your strongest assets and the skills you want to develop. What is your plan for practicing the skills you need?

Situation Exercise 18.3. Creating a Script for Your Conversation. Develop a script of the toughest parts of the conversation with your receiver, using Grid TB 4 as a guide. Make your receiver realistic in his or her reactions. Write the exact words that you and your receiver might use (don't just generally describe or talk about these words). Also include statements that indicate tone, almost as if you were writing a play. The goal is to record a troublesome exchange. Then critique and change the script. Review it with a colleague for ideas. If this person is familiar with the receiver's usual reactions, so much the better.

You	Your Receiver
Your words: What you would say and how you would say it. Make your words exact enough to use quotation marks. Add a comment describing your tone of voice, such as "(calmly)." Your response to your receiver's comment And so on	Your receiver's words and tone in response to what you just said And so on

Grid TB 4. Writing a Script.

Situation Exercise 18.4. Your Affirmations for a Tough Case. Review General Exercises 4.2 and 4.3. Add to or change your affirmations based on your specific tough case. You might use statements about your skills, your character, or your beliefs.

Situation Exercise 18.5. Your Level of Acceptance. Take a look at Grid 18.1. Use the questions listed to answer yes or no for acceptance of the situation, of yourself as a messenger, and of your receiver. Avoid "maybes"—acceptance isn't a maybe thing. Be sure to respond to the "why or why not" questions.

Now decide if your answers mean that you are high or low on acceptance and record your thoughts. How will this influence your decision to speak up?

CHAPTER NINETEEN:
TALK WITH YOUR RECEIVER IN A TOUGH CASE

Situation Exercise 19.1. Improving Your Script. Look back over the script developed for Situation Exercise 18.3 (or do it now). Based on the tips presented in Chapter Nineteen, do you see some additional ways to express yourself that might be helpful to the conversation? Specifically look for places in your script to:

- Restate your purpose

- Make observations about what you see happening

- Share your feelings

- Listen without judgment and paraphrase

- Share negative assumptions

- Ask for feedback

Situation Exercise 19.2. Discussing Your Negative Assumptions. Whether you actually intend to do so or not, carefully plan words you can use to share your negative assumptions. Carefully look over the examples presented in the chapter. Then draft several versions of how you might communicate to your receiver about your own negative assumptions. Describe the tone of voice you will need to use.

Situation Exercise 19.3. Asking for Your Receiver's Assumptions. Draft several phrases you might use to ask your receiver about his or her negative assumptions about you. See "When You Are the Receiver of Tough News" later in the Messenger's Tool Box for additional details.

CHAPTER TWENTY: HOW DID IT GO? WHAT DID YOU LEARN?

Situation Exercise 20.1. Should You Evaluate Your Speaking-Up Experiences? Given your situation and experience, do you think it would be valuable for you to assess how your speaking-up situation has gone? Why or why not? What feelings do you have about your answer to these questions?

General Exercise 20.2. Your Reasons for Wanting to Improve. If you decide to get better at bringing forward tough news, which of the three reasons listed below is most important to you? Do you have other reasons for wanting to get better? What are they?

1. Enhancing personal integrity and self-worth

2. Reducing frustration and increasing pleasure in the work environment

3. Contributing to the strength and health of organizations

Situation Exercise 20.3. Answer the Four Questions. Use Grid TB 5 as a template for recording your answers to the questions listed in the chapter. As you work with the grid, identify your learnings and how you might put them to use in the future—either by building on them or by doing things differently in order to improve. Be sure to include follow-up information, for example, a need to have another conversation with the receiver.

Situation Exercise 20.4. Thinking About "Maybes" and "No's." Here are additional questions worth considering if you answered the four questions "Maybe" or "No." "Maybe" and "No" answers can reveal insights about the complexity of your speaking-up situation. The additional questions further your exploration.

Did I Do the Right Thing?

- What were your honest intentions? To what degree was your motivation to help? What benefits were you after—for yourself, the organization, and your receiver?

- Would more preparation have caused you to decide not to speak up? If so, what might that have been?

- Would another person in your shoes have chosen to speak up? Why or why not?

Did I Do It Well?

- As you replay the conversation in your head, what aspects of your approach or behavior could have been improved? If you could redo those aspects, how would you like to see yourself behave?

- Of all the things you might do to improve your effectiveness as a messenger in this situation, what is the one thing that seems most important to change? Why is this so important?

Question	Answer	In the Future
Did I do the right thing?	_____ Yes Maybe No Data:	Celebrate and build on: Do differently: Follow up:
Did I do it well?	_____ Yes Maybe No Data:	Celebrate and build on: Do differently: Follow up:
Was it well received?	_____ Yes Maybe No Data:	Celebrate and build on: Do differently: Follow up:
Did it make a positive difference?	_____ Yes Maybe No Data:	Celebrate and build on: Do differently: Follow up:

Grid TB 5. Evaluating Your Situation.

Was It Well Received?

- If you have ongoing contact with your receiver, you may be able to assess her or his reaction to your message by the nature of later interactions. Can you gather any indications from observing the receiver's behavior?

- If you experienced a negative reaction during your conversation and your receiver clearly disagreed with aspects of your message, do you understand the reasons behind these reactions? If this was not discussed during the conversation, do you have any way to talk with your receiver after the fact, in order to better understand his or her point of view?

Did It Make a Positive Difference?

- If your receiver had a negative response to your request for action, how else might you pursue your concerns?

- Are any less obvious positive results connected to your conversation—for example, gaining new information that will help you in your job or the satisfaction that comes from having acted in accord with your values?

- If nothing results from your efforts, how disappointing is that to you? Can some positive learnings, rather than ones that reinforce cynicism, come from this experience? If so, what might they be? How can you apply them the next time you speak up?

- If you know there have been, or sense there will be, repercussions for you or others as a result of your speaking up, how much of a problem will that be for you? Why will this be the case? Is there anything you can do to minimize the impact of these repercussions?

CHAPTER TWENTY-ONE:
THE MESSENGER'S TRANSFORMATION

General Exercise 21.1. Your Past and Current Beliefs. Create a grid describing your own past and current beliefs, using Grid 21.1 as a model. You can use your grid to document any kind of personal transformation, not just one related to speaking up. But if you feel that you have already turned several corners as a messenger, use it now to record your insights and the changes in your beliefs.

Story Exercise 21.2. Sarah's Transformation. What do you believe are the most important ways in which Sarah Eastland offers a model for personal transformation? What appear to be the advantages and downsides of her experience? What relevance does this analysis have to your own situation or future directions?

General Exercise 21.3. Where Are You in the Transformation Process? Look at the phases and action steps described for the messenger's journey of transformation. Which of these phases best represents where you are today? How can you use the suggested action steps to move to the next phase? Do you have a different view of the stages of personal transformation?

CHAPTER TWENTY-TWO:
CHANGING THE ORGANIZATION BY SPEAKING UP

General Exercise 22.1. Four Suggestions for Action. Four suggestions for action are defined for messengers who want to help change their organization. Based on your skills and personal style, which of these actions would be the most comfortable for you? Which would be the least comfortable? Why?

General Exercise 22.2. The Chain of Impacts. Describe the chain of impacts as it applies to your organization. Is it positive or negative? Do certain situations or events come to mind as you follow the paths toward success or decline? Why do these situations stand out?

General Exercise 22.3. The "Critical Mass." Is a critical mass of messengers being built in your organization? What is your role as a leader of this change?

BASIC COMMUNICATION SKILLS

As a skillful and successful messenger, you must send your message and respond to your receiver with *clarity and impact.* This section is a review of the interpersonal communication skills that will help you to move through a conversation with your receiver in an open, direct, and unambiguous way.

These skills, once learned, are applicable anywhere, at any time, in conversations of all types. However, they are particularly important when you need to put sensitive topics on the table and want to get through the discussion with your integrity and relationship with your receiver intact. Some of these techniques and concepts will be familiar to you if you have attended workshops or read books on communication.

The order in which the skills are described does not express a sequence of how a messenger might use them in a conversation with a receiver. In a discussion, you can use the skills whenever you need to.

LISTENING

A good listener focuses completely on the person who is doing the talking. Good listeners say things that cause the person who is speaking to go further with his or her thoughts. Paraphrasing, asking clarifying questions, and asking informational questions are the basic ways to find out more about what the speaker is saying. In emotional situations, good listening helps a person to gain insight about what someone else really means. It also allows time to think before jumping in with a response. Here are some examples of each tool and a set of phrases that demonstrate each one.

Paraphrasing. Paraphrasing is putting into your own words what you hear another person say. It is given in the form of a statement, not a question:

> "Let me make sure I understood what you were saying, Hans. Your point is that . . ."
>
> "So, from your perspective, we need to . . ."
>
> "You believe that in order to be successful, our work group should . . ."
>
> "You're feeling _____ and you want me to . . ."

Asking Clarifying Questions. These are questions that seek clarification about the meaning of what the other person has just said; they frequently clarify the *degree* of what the other person is talking about:

> "How much do you think upper management is aware of this problem?"
>
> "If you could replay the situation, how would you like me to behave differently?"
>
> "How big a concern is this to you, given everything else you've got on your plate?"
>
> "How does this situation compare to others you've experienced?"

Asking Informational Questions. Informational questions ask for new or additional facts, ideas, or perspectives:

> "Can you give me an example that will help me to understand what you mean?"

"What do you think is causing all this?"

"Has something specific led you to this conclusion?"

"What do we do next?"

MAKING ASSERTIVE STATEMENTS

Assertive statements are confident, clear statements or questions that let the other person know what you want or need. They are not confrontational. They put no one down, not the others who are involved and not the person who is speaking. They are usually short and easy to understand. They put your issue firmly on the table for discussion and convey the idea that you know what you want.

Making Statements of Wants, Needs, and Intentions. These are concisely worded statements that let others know what you desire, require, or intend to do:

"I want . . ."

"I intend . . ."

"I need . . ."

"Next, I plan to . . ."

Asking for Help or Support. These questions clearly ask others for some specific type of assistance; they are often combined with assertive statements:

"Will you be able to meet me early so we can plan what we're going to do?"

"I need to get better prepared on this computer program. Can you help me find a resource?"

"Do you have the time to give me the coaching I need?"

"I'd like to follow up on your suggestion to talk with Jamila. Can you help me get in to see her?"

MAKING OBSERVATIONS IN NEUTRAL, NONJUDGMENTAL WAYS

One of the keys to staying focused and calm during messenger situations is to make neutral observations about people's behavior (your own included), the points that are being made, and the tone of the conversation. These observations mostly come in the form of statements, which are often paraphrases. They are sometimes followed by a question.

It is best to use words that are descriptive, yet not emotionally charged, because they may trigger defensiveness on the part of the other person. It is also important to maintain an open, nonjudgmental tone of voice when offering an observation. A person may have chosen neutral words for an observation, but if her or his tone of voice is sarcastic or judgmental, the neutrality will be lost. Examples, some effective and some less effective, are contrasted below.

More Effective

"Shareef, you seem upset by what I've just told you. Can you help me understand why you have reacted in this way?"

Less Effective

"Shareef, you really flew off the handle when I brought this up. Is something wrong with you?"

More Effective

"I'm having a hard time following what you are saying, Jenny. Let me see if I can paraphrase your point. You are concerned about . . ."

Less Effective

"It seems to me that you're making this overly complex, Jenny. You've lost me again!"

More Effective

"Larry, I'm just too uncomfortable to go on right now with this conversation. Can we take a break?"

Less Effective

"For crying out loud, Larry! Can't you see what it's like to be attacked like this? Damn it—back off!"

MAKING SELF-DISCLOSING STATEMENTS
ABOUT YOUR OWN FEELINGS

Self-disclosure means sharing something that is somewhat private about yourself with another person. The ability to be self-disclosing about feelings is an important interpersonal skill. Without it, communication about complex issues remains at the intellectual level and often feels empty, or not real. Because most of the difficult messages you will bring forward as a messenger are complex and can have an emotional impact, it is helpful to know how to describe the emotions you experience while discussing your message. The more specific you can be, the more powerful the self-disclosing statement will be and the more likely it is that your discussions will carry personal meaning, in addition to taking care of a task.

When it comes to discussing feelings, sometimes all that messengers are able to muster is a statement like "I feel good (or bad) about this." But when you can go beyond the surface level, your listeners will gain more information and are much more likely to pay attention to what is going on inside you in the moment. Words that describe emotions that frequently come up in messenger conversations include *relieved, excited, renewed, grateful, encouraged, glad, supported, appreciated, overwhelmed, anxious, nervous, fearful, intimidated, frustrated, worried,* and *angry.*

Note that whenever a person uses the phrase "I feel that . . . ," he or she is *not* being self-disclosing about feelings. The word *that* changes the sentence from one about feelings into one about opinions. For example, compare the following three sets of responses:

"I feel that we should make a decision."

"I feel frustrated about the lack of a clear decision."

"I feel that you're confusing the issue."

"I'm angry. I believe the issues are confused."

"I feel that we're on the verge of a breakthrough."

"This is so exciting to me. We're truly at a breakthrough point!"

It is easy for people to mislead themselves and others with the "I feel that" phrase. It gives the illusion that a person is being self-disclosing about feelings when that is not actually the case. Statements that are revealing of emotions get straight to the point with the phrase "I feel _____," where the word *feel* is followed immediately by a word describing an emotion.

GIVING FEEDBACK

Most people have a hard time giving feedback. Even giving positive feedback is difficult for many. Critical feedback is particularly hard to give in the moment, when conversation is moving quickly and issues are potentially emotional. In such situations, it is easy to slide into criticizing and blaming, which can easily lead to defensiveness and end attempts to constructively discuss a problem or concern.

The technique that works best in such situations is based upon the "I-message" described years ago by Thomas Gordon.[1] As you review the components of the I-message below, you'll see that it combines aspects of assertive and self-disclosing statements and observations. It has three basic aspects:

1. A neutral description of the *behavior* about which you are giving feedback

2. A self-disclosing statement about *your feelings* triggered by the behavior

3. An assertive statement of the *impact* of the behavior

Here are some examples of how it is used. Notice how the three supplemental skills work together to present information to someone in a constructive, nonblaming way:

> "Maria, I feel very supported when you take the time to see me on such a busy day. Your willingness to hear what I have to say makes it a whole lot easier to raise a complicated issue that's really getting in my way."

---

1. Thomas Gordon, *Parent Effectiveness Training: The Tested Way to Raise Responsible Children* (New York: Peter H. Wyden, 1970).

- *Behavior of the other person:* Taking the time to get together

- *Feelings of the person giving feedback:* Supported

- *Impact of the behavior:* Makes it easier to bring up a complicated subject

"Todd, when you raise your voice and keep asking me questions, I really feel on the spot. It makes it hard for me to think clearly and give you my best answers."

- *Behavior of the other person:* Raising the voice and asking questions

- *Feelings of the person giving feedback:* On the spot

- *Impact of the behavior:* Makes it hard to give the best answers

"Bill, when you keep looking at your watch, I feel awkward, like this isn't a good time for you, or you aren't really interested in what I have to say. This makes it harder for me to give you the information you've asked for, since it isn't positive news."

- *Behavior of the other person:* Looking at watch

- *Feelings of the person giving feedback:* Awkward

- *Impact of the behavior:* Makes it harder to give the requested information

ASKING FOR AND HEARING FEEDBACK

Effective messengers need to be ready to ask for and hear feedback from their receivers. Once a messenger begins a conversation, it is impossible to predict how it will evolve. If, in addition to bringing up your ideas, you want to discuss them in an open, positive way with your receiver, you may well need to ask for feedback at some point during the conversation.

Reasons Why You Might Want to Ask for Feedback. The following circumstances might indicate the need for such a request:

- In exploring the causes or contributing factors to the issue you've brought up, you sense that your behavior might be part of the problem; you may need to find out if your receiver has the same impression.

- If your receiver seems resistive or disinterested, you may need to ask for feedback on how you are presenting your message; perhaps your method of delivering the message is getting in the way of the receiver's understanding your point.

- If your receiver has a much stronger or different emotional reaction than you anticipated or than seems reasonable, you might ask if you have done something to upset the receiver, outside of bringing the message forward.

- At the end of the conversation, you may want to ask for the receiver's reaction to the discussion you've had, the way in which you brought the subject up, or the impact the conversation might have had on your relationship.

How to Ask for Feedback. Asking for feedback relies on making observations, self-disclosing statements, and assertive statements and asking clarifying questions. These basic skills are combined in various ways, depending on what prompts you to ask for feedback. Here are examples of the way you might ask for feedback for each of the circumstances we've just identified.

When you think you might be part of the problem:

> "Ann, as we've been talking about the problem with Mei Ming and how she's doing her job, I just realized that I may well have contributed to the situation by not being more direct with her. Do you have any thoughts on that for me?"

When you think your method of bringing up your subject is getting in the way of the receiver's hearing your point:

> "Paul, I'm feeling very awkward about bringing this whole thing up. I don't know that I'm doing a very good job of it. Am I making sense to you? It's really important to me that you understand why I'm here."

When your receiver's reaction is much stronger than you anticipated:

> "Gosh, Marta, you seem much more upset than I thought you might be. Have I done something—aside from bringing this information up—that's troubling you? I'd really like to know."

When you want to know how the receiver is reacting at the end of your conversation:

> "Before we break up, Jack, can I ask how you're feeling about our conversation? I know that this hasn't been easy or much fun for you. Could I have been more helpful?"

How to Hear Critical Feedback. When you ask for feedback, you have to be ready to be open and hear whatever your receiver has to say, even if it is critical of your behavior or your intentions. This can be tough to do. The main strategy is to use the listening skills of paraphrasing and asking questions to clarify what the receiver is saying or to seek more information. Paraphrasing is particularly helpful as a means of giving you time to take in what the receiver has said before you say anything back. By listening, you give yourself time to take a deep breath and think about what you truly want to say next, rather than simply reacting in a way that could be seen as defensive.

The paraphrase also lets the person giving you the feedback know that you understand the point being made; if you have missed it, then the paraphrase enables the misunderstanding to be cleared up quickly. Additionally, self-disclosing statements will help your receiver know how you are reacting on an emotional level; they also allow you a means of releasing some of the stress that can come with tough feedback. The examples that follow demonstrate the use of each skill, using the same vignettes as in the previous section on asking for feedback.

When you think you might be part of the problem:

> Messenger: "So, Ann, you're saying that you think my concerns with Mei Ming actually started when I didn't tell her exactly what we needed from her at the beginning of this project, and that this

whole thing could have been prevented if I'd handled it differently." (pause to see if paraphrase is correct)

Ann: "That's right."

Messenger: "Wow. That's a lot to take in. I had no idea that I might have been at the source of this thing. Can you tell me how you've reached that conclusion?"

When you think that your method of bringing up your subject is getting in the way of the receiver's hearing your point:

Messenger: "From what you're saying, Paul, it sounds like it would help you out if I gave you an example of what I'm talking about, rather than to keep telling you how I feel about things."

Paul: "It would make a lot more sense to me if you could. I'm not sure I really understand what you're talking about."

Messenger: "Fair enough. Let me see if I can be more concrete. This first came up for me last month when . . ."

When your receiver's reaction is much stronger than you anticipated:

Messenger: "Marta, thanks for telling me this. You're right. I didn't know that you saw me as complaining about things whenever I came to see you. I can see where just seeing me walk in the door could put you on edge. Would it be better if I came back later?"

When you want to know how the receiver is reacting at the end of your conversation:

Messenger: "Jack, I really appreciate your being straight with me. I was pretty stirred up when we started the conversation. That must have made it harder for you to understand what I was really trying to say. Can you tell me how I could have approached you in a better way? I'd like to know in case this sort of thing ever comes up again."

MANAGING YOUR EMOTIONS

It is helpful to stay calm during your conversation with your messenger. Above all, it is important not to become defensive or attack your receiver. At such moments, you can lose your clarity and impact and run the risk of damaging your relationship with your receiver. It is this "out-of-control" scene that worries so many people and keeps them from coming forward with their concerns and good ideas. For these reasons, it is well worth the effort to develop the ability to manage your emotions during stressful communications with receivers.

Managing Emotions by Acknowledging Them. Remember that managing your emotions does not mean *hiding* them. In fact, as you can see from some of the examples above, using self-disclosing statements as a means of acknowledging emotions, even ones of anger, frustration, or disappointment, can be effective. Describing your emotions requires you to slow down and think a bit about how you are reacting on the inside to the conversation you are having with your receiver. This also serves as a way to release at least a small amount of the tension you may be experiencing. For example:

"I feel frustrated about the lack of a clear decision."

"This makes me angry. I believe the issues are more complicated."

"Bjorn, when you keep working on your files while we talk, I feel discounted and am frustrated that you don't see this issue as being very important."

Matching Your Verbal and Nonverbal Communication. Messengers can cause their receivers to question their motivations and their truthfulness. They do this by saying words that are not matched by the nonverbal signals they send through their body language, tone of voice, and vocal inflection. This lack of connection between words and other signals typically conveys a strong sense of discomfort or dishonesty. Such messengers are often described as being phony, not being genuine, or, worst of all, being manipulative. These perceptions, whether correct or not, can make it very difficult for messengers to proceed successfully.

Two steps will help you to increase the match between your words and your nonverbal behavior. First, learn to identify and describe the emotions you are experiencing in the moment. Second, don't try to hide those emotions by denying your feelings or trying to mask them by behaving in other ways. For example:

- If you are nervous, don't try to be overly relaxed or in control.

- If you are sad or angry, don't smile when you are talking.

- If your receiver asks about the impact of a situation, don't minimize its effect.

Sometimes, your emotions may be so strong that you cannot behave as you would like. This happens to almost everyone at some time. If you sense that your anger, frustration, confusion, or fear are about to trigger behavior that is highly emotional and reactive, ask for a time-out. Make a statement that is both assertive and self-disclosing, for example, "Phyllis, you've just told me things that have taken me completely by surprise. I'd like to take ten minutes to get my feelings sorted out before we continue."

Understanding and becoming competent at using these skills are central to helping you communicate your difficult messages to others at work. Additionally, the suggestions outlined here can apply directly to other situations—at home, in community groups, and with friends and neighbors. The benefits of mastering these skills can be great. They represent a core skill set for developing and maintaining positive relationships in all aspects of your life.

WHEN YOU ARE THE RECEIVER OF TOUGH NEWS

This book is devoted to helping you become a courageous messenger. There also may be times when you will want to be a courageous receiver—for example:

- When you find yourself asking for feedback during a conversation that you initiated as the messenger

- When someone else approaches you with a tough message

- When, as part of an ordinary conversation, you unexpectedly realize that you are in the middle of a discussion about a tough issue and that you are in the receiver's role

Whether you are a leader, an associate, a team member, a colleague, or a friend, you will have many opportunities to be a receiver of tough news.

Here are a few tips on how to make the most of this role, for yourself, your messenger, and your organization. For more about words you can use to ask for feedback and for other important skills referred to in this summary, turn to "Basic Communication Skills" earlier in the Messenger's Tool Box.

Slow down and focus on communicating with the messenger. Notice right away that you are entering a messenger-receiver dialogue and move toward, rather than away from, the messenger. Let the person know that you are ready to listen through verbal and nonverbal signals. If you feel that environmental barriers might interfere, such as a large desk between you or an open door, overcome them. Put aside other issues so that you can attend fully to your messenger. If the time is not right, agree on another time to meet as soon as possible.

Now and later, thank the messenger for taking the time, and the risk, to approach you. A few words of appreciation help to cut the tension and reduce the worries your messenger may bring. This sets the stage for a more open dialogue. Don't forget to thank the messenger after the message, too.

Allow the messenger to express the message. Unexpected messages may result in defensive reactions on your part. You might be tempted to interrupt with questions or an evaluation of the points the messenger presents. Be aware of your emotional reactions and how they can inadvertently create an environment of tension and closed communication. Use a tone of openness to welcome information, even if the message seems to be an uncomfortable one to hear or the messenger's manner is tense or emotional. Staying calm yourself often helps the messenger to be more relaxed.

Ask questions when you don't understand. Don't sit back in silence if you are unclear about what the messenger is telling you. Use a variety of communication tools, such as paraphrases and open-ended and clarifying questions, to get more information. Ask for examples of issues or problems, but be careful not to interrogate the messenger. Rather, work *with* the messenger to mutually understand:

- The situation and its effects
- The messenger's personal reactions to the situation, and your own
- The causes of the situation
- The messenger's request and what needs to be done

Have a conversation. Foster a full exploration of the issues with the messenger. Without defending or arguing, talk about your own perspectives, information, and experiences. Share as openly as you can some aspects of your feelings about the message that has been brought forward. If you disagree with a comment, say so, expressing yourself in a way that is likely to encourage further exploration of the point. Then focus on finding common ground and deciding on what can be jointly accomplished to improve the circumstances.

Make it okay to talk about your behavior and your relationship with the messenger if they appear to be involved. Invite the messenger's candid observations. Explain your desire for personal growth and improvement and your willingness to hear the messenger's perspectives. Let the messenger know that you value his or her opinion and that you can appreciate the messenger's feelings in the situation.

During the conversation, invite two kinds of data: (1) the perceptions and opinions that the messenger has of you and (2) the messenger's observations of the behavior that has led to these perceptions. For example, you might say:

> "I appreciate your telling me that people think I don't seem to be very interested in the division's customer service project. (a perception) Can you tell me more—what I've specifically done or not done that's led to this conclusion?" (behaviors)

Evaluate what you hear carefully. Think about the connection between the behaviors and the perceptions. Whether or not this connection makes perfect sense to you, decide if personal change is in order.

Be aware of any negative assumptions that you may be making about the messenger. Notice, in particular, assumptions about why the messenger has approached you or is choosing to give you some hard news in the moment. If you find that you are privately drawing negative conclusions about what has motivated the messenger, ask the person to describe his or her reasons directly.

As a product of the conversation, make specific agreements and follow through with them. Turn new information and understandings into action steps that both you and the messenger can agree to. Take a collaborative approach, where both sides may have responsibilities they need to act on. Get back together at a predetermined time to evaluate progress or decide if the issues have been resolved.

Practice. Accomplishing the points outlined above depends on acceptance of yourself and others—and practice. Being an effective receiver is also an everyday act of courage. Here are three additional suggestions that will help you to become more approachable in everyday situations and more skilled in responding to sensitive issues:

1. *Encourage others to express themselves, their personal feelings, and their perspectives.* Ask about feelings as well as facts. Don't be satisfied with abstract discussions that circle the tough issues. In order to get to the core of the tough news, explore underlying causes and assumptions. This type of probing will illuminate the work outcomes, working relationships, or personal behavior at the heart of the message.

2. *Ask for feedback before any messenger has approached you.* Become comfortable and skilled in surfacing the issues that have to do with you—with your style, reputation, and performance. On a frequent basis, ask others for their observations of what you could do differently to improve your performance and working relationships. Let people know how you have responded to their feedback.

3. *Acknowledge how you defend yourself.* Everyone has the potential to strike back unfairly when negative ideas or feedback are laid on the doorstep. Recognize that you may be capable of exacting your own, perhaps subtle or unconscious, brand of retaliation when others' points come too close. Acknowledge and understand this behavior, whether it is something that happens in the moment or occurs later, as in holding a grudge. Notice when this behavior may be happening so that you can check its impact on others.

Putting these general suggestions into place can have payoffs in terms of powerful problem solving and increased trust. More than messengers, receivers are in a key position to change the dynamics of a conversation. Their willingness to hear tough news can make all the difference.

WHEN YOU CANNOT DELIVER YOUR MESSAGE IN PERSON

New communication tools are helping people to cope with the changes in the nature of work and in the way organizations are structured. Desktop video links, televideo conferencing, E-mail, voice mail, fax machines, teleconferencing, and the ever-present telephone are available in some combination to most people at work.

When you are faced with the need to speak up about difficult issues, the basic advice presented in this book remains the same. Make every effort to find a way to do so face-to-face with your receiver, because the emotional and personal *context* of communication is extremely important. Context is the meaning that surrounds the spoken words in a conversation. This extra portion of meaning comes from observing such things as body language, tone of voice, and vocal inflection. Much of the communication that takes place during a face-to-face conversation comes in this way. Without this context, the opportunities for misunderstandings are greatly magnified. This can be particularly true when you have no existing trust-based relationship with your receiver. Speaking up about the tough issues at work can be challenging enough without this additional handicap.

THE ELECTRONIC MESSENGER

It is not always possible to follow our advice about face-to-face communication. The goal then is to select a tool that offers the greatest opportunity to successfully convey your message to the receiver. Visual options such as desktop video and televideo conferencing present the best chance for this communication. Interactive audio links such as the telephone and group teleconferencing make up the next best option. They allow the tone of voice and inflection to come through, are in real time, and are interactive.

Voice mail is less effective because it is a one-way medium. The message is delivered with some vocal context but your receiver does not have the ability to respond, seek clarification, or ask for more information in the moment. Voice mail often has time limits, making it difficult to communicate a complex, sensitive message. The delay in response may complicate an urgent or immediate issue.

In most cases, the medium that is least effective for communicating a difficult message is E-mail via computer. E-mail usually offers the least amount of context to the receiver. It is also one-way and does not occur in real time.

E-mail also presents a problem because of one of its major advantages: its ease of use. Many people we have interviewed have mentioned the danger of sitting down in the seemingly private environment of their work space and dashing off a quick message expressing much more frustration or anger than they would ever express in person. They speak of hitting their E-mail "Send" button without thinking through their message or its potential impact. The tales of regret and embarrassment are many and are often compounded by the fact that E-mail is also one of the least private and secure modes to use in communicating difficult messages. Your mail can end up on every networked screen in the company.

E-mail plays an important role in today's business organizations. It is very effective for communicating many kinds of things, including:

- Sending fact-based information

- Exploring ideas

- Keeping a group of people in the information "loop"

- Creating a written record of communications

- Sending time-valued information

263

It is less effective in meeting other needs, including:

- Resolving conflict
- Dealing with feelings or emotionally charged subjects
- Negotiating back and forth
- Addressing complex topics
- Fulfilling a need for private, secure communication

Experienced E-mail users have developed methods of adding some of the emotional context with the use of type case and symbols. For example, CAPITAL LETTERS denote a loud or strong statement. Combining a colon and a parenthesis can indicate pleasure, :), or sadness, :(. This can be helpful for receivers who have little to go on but words to figure out what is really being communicated. However, these methods do not generally overcome the inherent limitations of the medium in communicating tough issues.

TIPS FOR THE ELECTRONIC MESSENGER

Think twice.   Be careful about picking up the phone or opening your E-mail screen when you are upset. Being a skilled and successful messenger is challenging enough when you are prepared and relatively calm. It is almost impossible when you are angry or frustrated. If writing it down helps you to blow off steam, do so, but stop and think twice before sending your message.

Choose your media carefully.   If you have the option, seek the most interactive and visual of the media for the difficult messages. It may pay to delay your message until you find a better alternative. This is particularly true if your only option at the moment is E-mail and you do not have an established relationship with your receiver. In some cases, a written message can be seen as more intimidating or unfriendly than one delivered in another way. Selection of an audio or video medium could help you to avoid conveying one of those impressions.

Be aware of your receiver's media comfort zone.   Your ability to be successful may be determined by your receiver's comfort with the medium you are using. You may be very skilled and comfortable with various forms of electronic media, but your receiver may not. Be careful not to make assumptions about how well another person may interact with your choice. Many people in the workplace did not grow up with these tools and are uneasy using them, especially when the topic is a difficult one. Your communication may need to acknowledge this. Ask whether your receiver would prefer another means of conducting the discussion.

Think ahead. Have data, strategies, outcomes—perhaps even a script—prepared and in place when you begin your communication. The electronic messenger is advised to prepare even more thoroughly than when planning for a face-to-face encounter.

Help the receiver to understand the missing context. Compensate for the missing personal and emotional context of live conversations. Consider being more descriptive about how the situation affects you and your feelings than you might normally be. If you are communicating by E-mail, consider using the accepted symbols to add some small level of emotional context to your written message.

Know the local rules of the road. Know what your organization or your receiver's organization has in place as guidelines for using any of the various electronic media. Many organizations have developed E-mail or teleconferencing protocols that are designed to help the communication process. Commonly accepted forms of network etiquette, or "netiquette," may be helpful to know and use. Employ these protocols and forms of etiquette when you can.

Be aware of privacy and confidentiality issues. Electronic media generally do not offer privacy or confidentiality to you or your message. With all the media, except perhaps the telephone, a written or recorded version of your communication may well exist. In addition, with E-mail and some voice mail systems, a message can be broadcast company-wide, or even worldwide, with the push of a button. In the case of video or audio hookups, others who are known or unknown to you may be present as you convey your message. This may or may not be a concern, but as a messenger, you must be aware of the potential.

SUMMARY OF TIPS FOR MESSENGERS

CHAPTER ELEVEN:
GET READY FOR THE CONVERSATION

Choose a good time and situation in which to deliver your message; do so as soon as possible.

Set up enough time to be able to fully discuss your message.

Spend time thinking about and preparing for your conversation.

Take your receiver's communication style into consideration.

Be sensitive to how your receiver is likely to react to your message, as well as to other things he or she might be facing at the same time.

Don't assume that your receiver cannot handle or is not interested in your message.

CHAPTER TWELVE:
OPEN THE CONVERSATION

Express appreciation for the time to meet with the receiver and your hopes for a two-way exchange of ideas and viewpoints.

Open the conversation in a calm and tactful manner, quickly becoming more direct about your message.

Have a sincere attitude and tone.

CHAPTER THIRTEEN:
PRESENT YOUR MESSAGE AND MOTIVATION

Describe the problem or your concerns in terms that are important to the receiver.

State clearly why you have raised your concerns and want to talk about them.

State clearly what you need, want, hope for, or expect from your receiver.

Don't whine, dump, or avoid responsibility; when you are involved in the problem, acknowledge your role.

Don't overstate or exaggerate the problem by making insupportable or extreme comments; describe the factual impacts as accurately as you can.

Don't state your message or motivation in a voice that is too loud or too soft.

Don't undermine the sincerity of your message and motivation through jokes, sarcasm, or innuendo.

Don't undermine the power of your message and motivation through self-deprecating remarks and apologies.

CHAPTER FOURTEEN:
TALK ABOUT YOUR MESSAGE WITH YOUR RECEIVER

Listen carefully to the receiver's perspective about your message, especially if she or he seems to resist what you are saying or becomes emotional.

If you can, offer additional information to help the receiver understand the importance of the issues to you.

Don't make negative assumptions about your receiver's or others' intentions.

267

Use neutral words to describe the behavior or circumstances that are creating problems, not phrases that communicate blame.

Stay open-minded to what your receiver says; don't discount the receiver's reaction to your message or jump to conclusions based on your own biases.

If you find yourself getting emotional, describe your feelings rather than acting them out.

Look for opportunities to ask for feedback about your message or your manner of bringing it forward.

If it is appropriate, discuss what you are willing to do or what you have already been doing to deal with the situation.

If possible, offer ideas about what to do next.

CHAPTER FIFTEEN: WRAP UP THE CONVERSATION

Summarize understandings, agreements, and any commitments for action.

Reinforce your reason for bringing your message forward.

If the conversation was difficult, acknowledge the emotional side of what happened.

End the conversation graciously.

CHAPTER SIXTEEN: FOLLOW THROUGH

Make sure that you do what you told your receiver you would do.

Stay practical and flexible; recognize that your plans may need to change or be renegotiated as other events take place.

If your receiver promised to do things and you believe that this has not happened, voice your concerns.

If your receiver does not follow through, don't make negative assumptions about his or her intentions or jump to conclusions about why the expected action did not take place.

CHAPTER EIGHTEEN: GET READY FOR A TOUGH CASE

Understand the emotions you have about speaking up in this tough case.

Carefully assess your communication skills and ability to apply recommended strategies.

Rehearse the way you will express your message, motivation, or other things you might say if your receiver becomes emotional or resistive.

Use affirmations to help you approach your conversation with a constructive and confident attitude.

Focus on acceptance.

If you find yourself low on acceptance, rethink your decision to speak up.

CHAPTER NINETEEN: TALK WITH YOUR RECEIVER IN A TOUGH CASE

Remember your purpose.

Make observations about the dynamics of what you see happening.

Share your feelings.

Listen completely to the other person without judgment.

Share your negative assumptions.

Ask for feedback about the negative assumptions your receiver may have about you.

Reschedule or extend the discussion.

Engage a third party.

INDEX